KT-198-657

THE CULTURAL HISTORY OF THE
PHARAOHS

TEXT AND PHOTOGRAPHS
BY HENRI STIERLIN

30130504256545

STL
CR

932
STI

ESSEX COUNTY LIBRARY

Cover

The gold mask of Tutankhamen's mummy, dating from 1345 B.C., found in his tomb in the Valley of the Kings. On the forehead the cobra and vulture insignia, symbolizing Upper and Lower Egypt. A false beard, attribute of the gods, adorns the chin.

Endpapers

The most tremendous monument in the history of mankind, the great pyramid of Cheops at Giza. Built at the dawn of Egyptian civilization, it includes a sum total of six million tons of building materials.

Title page

Tutankhamen's solid gold coffin, dating from 1345 B.C. and discovered in 1922 by Howard Carter in the Valley of the Kings. It is 187 cm (74 in) long. The ruler is depicted as the god Osiris. His arms folded across his chest hold the whip and sceptre, insignia of dominion. This admirable sarcophagus enriched with enamel inlays and coloured stones, represents the king enfolded in the protective wings of the tutelary vulture and cobra, symbols of Upper and Lower Egypt.

Photo credits

The 150 colour photographs that illustrate this work were all provided by Henri Stierlin, Geneva, except for the following documents:
Yvan Butler, Geneva, title page and p. 18 bottom, 19, 48, 49, 50 top, 51, 52, 53, 54, 55, 63 and 64 top.
Maurice Babey, Basle (Ziolo, Paris), p. 39 bottom, 44 bottom and 45.
Hans Hinz, Basle (Office du Livre, Fribourg), p. 44 top.
All the works belonging to the Treasure of Tutankhamen were photographed with the permission of the Cairo Museum. The Treasure of Byblos was photographed with the permission of the Beyrouth Museum of Archaeology. The author and photographer is most grateful to the Egyptian authorities and in particular to the Ministry of Tourism at Cairo for the cordial assistance given him during his expeditions in the Egyptian Arab Republic.

All rights reserved.
© *Agence Internationale d'Edition Jean-François Gonthier,*
1009 Pully (Switzerland), 1978.
This edition: Edito-Service S.A., Geneva, (Switzerland), 1983.
Translated by Erika Abrams.

ISBN 2-8302-0601-0
13 089 001

Printed in Italy

© *This edition Aurum Press Ltd.*
Published in 1983 in the U.K. and Commonwealt by Aurum Press Ltd. 33 Museum Street, London WC1. All rights reserved. No part of this book may be reproduced in any form or by any electronic or mechanical means, including information storage and retrieval systems, without written permission from the publisher.

ISBN 0-906053-51-X

DE 33538

932 STI

THE CULTURAL HISTORY OF THE
PHARAOHS

COLLEGE LIBRARY
COLLEGE OF TECHNOLOGY
CARNARVON ROAD
SOUTHEND-ON-SEA, ESSEX

Contents

The Egyptian Miracle

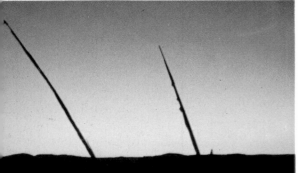

Egypt's sole source of life: the Nile. Its waters flow down from the great lakes of tropical Africa and the Abyssinian mountains, 4000 miles (6500 km) from the river's mouth which forms a delta on the Mediterranean. The Nile is also Egypt's main channel of communication.

If it weren't for the Nile — the longest river in the Old World : 4000 miles (6500 km) — Egypt would not exist. The Egyptian Nile, last section of the river which flows down from the great lakes of Central Africa or the Abyssinian mountains, is an axis cutting across desert emptiness from south to north over a distance of 620 miles (1000 km) i.e., from Philae, on the First Cataract, to the Mediterranean. Near its mouth, it forms an immense delta. But almost the whole of its course forms a narrow corridor, nowhere broader than 19 miles (30 km) hemmed in by the Libyan cliffs and the eastern ridge.

This tremendous watercourse forcing its way through a desert as barren as the Sahara and converting the valley into a gigantic oasis, is the very essence of the Egyptian miracle. The river is indeed the only source of water. It alone makes life possible, for rainfall in Middle and Upper Egypt is minimal.

In addition to this long ribbon of arable land surrounded by rock and sand, Egypt comprises a chain of oases in the western desert and a vast depression watered by a natural branch of the Nile : the Fayyum, forming a gash in the desert south-west of the dividing line between the Valley and the Delta, where the river branches out.

During the Paleolithic period, up to the beginning of the Neolithic, the region experienced humid eras, with a flora and fauna similar to those of tropical Africa. But rainfall slowly diminished and finally disappeared. From that moment on, the valley was the only possible refuge, for animals as well as for humans. This gradual desiccation which transformed the surrounding areas into deserts drew towards the river inhabitants of the four corners of the ancient world. As far back as prehistoric times, Egypt was already peopled by extremely divergent human types : dolichocephalic and brachycephalic, Semitic tribes from Palestine and the Sinai peninsula, blacks who descended the Nile from the deep south, Mediterranean races and shepherds native of the Sahara.

For quite a while this heterogeneous population, split up into tribes, lived on the fringes of the valley. Violent seasonal floods ravaged the marshy lowlands, covered with luxuriant vegetation. Aboriginal prairies bordered on swamps. Ponds alternated with banks of black mud deposited by the receding waters.

In order to start a new more settled agricultural life, the inhabitants no longer satisfied with eking out a scanty existence as hunters and scavengers, had first to tame this land of marshes and jungles. It was a huge undertaking way beyond the means of a whole clan, let alone individuals. The creation of canals intended to drain away excess water or, on the contrary, to irrigate distant fields, the construction of levees and embankments protecting the villages of the primitive farmers from

Image of eternal Egypt: a mud-walled village in the shade of palm groves. Fertile fields stretch out as far as the eye can see, cut here and there by irrigation canals lined with trees.

The Nile Valley is hemmed in on both sides by deserts of sand and rock. We see here the hostile world of thirst, the realm of death reserved for the necropoleis.

7

The break of day on the Nile at Aswan, where the valley becomes so narrow that arable fields entirely disappear, giving place to the granite barrier composing the First Cataract. In the foreground, the island of Elephantine, former site of the Nilometer, employed for measuring the height reached by annual floods. On the horizon sand dunes overlook the landscape.

the inundation — all this required a collective effort, a hierarchical society, a unified structure subject to the authority of a centralised government. The true birth of Egypt coincided with the unification of the valley under the control of a sole ruler, the Pharaoh. This unification sanctioned the occupation of the country by a people adapted to the environment. Intensive agriculture provided sustenance for a large population.

In the Nile Valley, everything is governed by the inundation: when the river had not yet been dammed, Egypt was entirely dependent for her crops upon the height reached by the rising waters. The Nile begins to swell in mid-June, as if to counterbalance the summer drought. The full height is reached in August and September. When the flood does not submerge the more distant fields, the harvest is poor and famine threatens the Valley's population. If, on the contrary, the swollen waters are too tempetuous and the inundation too extensive, if the current carries away the dykes and embankments, everything must be rebuilt from scratch.

But the Nile is also the chief channel of communication for those residing on its banks. The river transports heavy building materials

The Nile in Nubia, near Abu Simbel: a chaotic universe of barren and jagged mountains borders the river.

A typical Egyptian village: Edfu in Upper Egypt, with its brick houses, flat roofs and inner courtyards. The Muslim minaret is the only innovation since the times of the Pharaohs.

from Upper to Lower Egypt. The fellahs (peasants) sail upon the canals in frail skiffs. Small papyrus and reed boats carry hunters into the marshes in search of game. Ferries cross over from one bank to the other; in Pharaonic times, there was no bridge over the river. The Nile is more than a mere source of irrigation. The Egyptians spend their lives in an intimate symbiosis with the river. All the year round, countless flotillas enliven the majestic waters of the Nile.

One of the greatest civilizations in the history of mankind shall take birth in these conditions favourable to the growth of a mighty agrarian society: a civilization destined to subsist for three and a half thousand years, from the dawn of history and the discovery of writing to the closing of the temple of Philae in A.D. 550, marking the death of a cultural system, a world view, an art.

The most striking aspect of this immense period extending from the first feeble steps to the ultimate efflorescence, is its unity, its coherency, its originality.

Egypt evolved as an island protected on all sides by a boundless sea of deserts.

The Old Kingdom: Birth and Blossom

The Pharaoh Zoser invented building in stone, about 2800 B.C.: detail of a fluted column at Saqqara, dating from twenty-two centuries before the birth of Greek civilization.

The civilization of Pharaonic Egypt seems to appear already formed about 3100 B.C., just as Minerva sprung already armed from Jupiter's brain. Once the strugglings of prehistory are resolved with technical developments in agriculture, basketry, pottery, weaving and irrigation, the perfecting of flint and polished stone tools, evolution makes a sudden bound forward.

In fact, the same progress can be observed almost simultaneously in the Mesopotamian basin and on the banks of the Nile with the Sumerians also making notable advances. While it seems quite likely that these two cradles of civilization came into contact in the 4th millenium B.C., it would nonetheless be rash to affirm that the influence was all one way. A Sumerian influence on Egypt has indeed often been put forth to explain the similarity of certain brick structures characterized by a façade adorned with redans. But the emergence of hieroglyphic script in the two basins (before Babylonian cuneiform) might also be explained by means of an Egyptian influence.

Be that as it may, the creation of a truly Egyptian style becomes apparent at the time of the unification of the Nile Valley under King Narmer, about 3000 B.C. Its specific features will remain unchanged for

three and a half milleniums. In this respect, the emblematic designs adorning the famous stone palettes, employed for grinding up malachite used as eye make-up, are quite revealing. We may already observe the typical Egyptian treatment of the human figure : head, hips, legs and feet in profile, eye and shoulders full-face. These deformations — we prefer to speak of a conceptual view aiming at an intelligible synthesis of the idea "man" — will continue with only slight variations throughout the Old, Middle and New Kingdom, up to the Ptolemaic and Roman periods.

So much for the figurative language of the plastic arts. But the Egyptians also elaborate a mode of writing. This notation, known as hieroglyphic, is the first script used by mankind. It marks man's entry into history. Henceforth a permanent memory exists for generations gone by to hand down their technical achievements and accounts of outstanding historical events to those that follow, as well as to record their great myths and rites. "Hieroglyph" is a Greek term meaning literally sacred carvings, sacerdotal carvings ; when the Greeks established their colonies in Egypt, this archaic script, dating from the dawn of history, was employed exclusively by the priests of the Nile Valley for the inscriptions graven on temple walls. The hieroglyphs were

The first pyramid in Egyptian civilization towers above Zoser's funerary complex : the Step Pyramid of Saqqara. Built forty-eight centuries ago, its six stages rise up to a height of 204 feet (61 m). On the left, a barrel-roofed chapel with engaged columns, recently restored by the archaeologist Philippe Lauer.

Left:
The wall surrounding Zoser's pyramid : it is 5420 feet (1650 m) round and is modelled on the fortifications of the city of the living at Memphis. In the centre, the portal gives access to a colonnade.

"Modernism" of mankind's first stone architecture: striking profile of the enclosure wall with neither crowning nor ornamental moulding.

Above:
View of the enclosure wall of Zoser's sepulchre at Saqqara: recess-panelling recalling bastions adorned with redans is modelled after the mud-brick constructions of the earliest Egyptian dynasties.

originally ideograms: ideas were represented by images mirroring the meaning, for example a cow, a bird, a boat, a tool, a crown. Later on the Egyptian alphabet became syllabic, a sort of rebus obtained by transliterating the sounds corresponding to the first terms portrayed. From this time forward, the system is essentially phonetic. Nevertheless, as in many Middle Eastern languages (Hebrew, Aramaic, Arabic, etc.), vowels are not noted. In the classic era, the hieroglyphic alphabet includes nearly 700 signs. During the last centuries of Pharaonic Egypt, their number exceeds 2000. The Egyptian alphabet has become a genuine cryptography. Hieroglyphic reads sometimes from top to bottom, sometimes from left to right, but sometimes also from right to left.

On the famous predynastic palettes, hieroglyphs are crude and scarce. They indicate no more than a name or title. But the technique of writing soon becomes more elaborate and the hieroglyphic script is flexible enough to set down important works such as the "Pyramid Texts" lining the burial chambers of Unas and Pepi, about 2400 B.C. These texts are composed of several thousand "verses", each one being a magic or sacred incantation intended to make easier the ruler's life in the hereafter.

Indeed, Egypt founds her civilization on essentially religious grounds. She displays a primordial concern for life after death. It is not without good reason that the Greeks called the Egyptians "the most devout of men". Their religion is a coalescence or amalgam of the tribal beliefs peculiar to the various ethnic groups that make up the valley's population. Cosmologies and rituals were combined and organized into a more or less coherent mythology whilst at the same time allowing each region to claim the supremacy of its own god. This religious unification, comparable to territorial unity of Upper and Lower Egypt, is the work of the Pharaoh, who is the earthly incarnation of the sovereign god and the vehicle of his manifestations.

Indeed, Pharaoh identifies himself with the divinity — Horus, Amun or Rē. Both during his lifetime and after his death, he occupies a

pre-eminent and exceptional place in society. He is the deity, the focal point of the entire Egyptian socio-religious system. The great monuments intended to guarantee life in the hereafter are erected for Pharaoh alone. The priests pray for him alone, officiate in his name and call down heavenly blessings on him and on the whole country. He is the head of the community but also partakes of the divinity and thus represents the mediator in the highest sense of the word. He alone can maintain the cosmic cycle and preserve world order.

These important advances bring Egypt out of the Neolithic period, accompanied by a most significant discovery: metallurgy. However, while the first dynasties master the use of bronze, they give up neither their lithic implements nor their carved stone vases, to say nothing of the hard stone (diorite, aragonite, gneiss, etc.) sledges employed for quarry-

At the very end of the vast colonnade leading into Zoser's funerary complex, the extraordinary fascicled columns, four pairs of which give access to the cobra courtyard (in the background). The architect Imhotep, who had not as yet attained an entire mastery of stonework, did not dare detach the columns employed in this revolutionary structure from the adjacent walls in which they are engaged.

Facing page:
Elegant engaged papyrus columns on the façade of Zoser's "Northern House". In the last days of Egyptian civilization, the author of this gigantic funerary complex, the brilliant architect Imhotep, was worshipped as a god.

One of the chapels lining the great ceremonial courtyard in Zoser's complex at Saqqara: the barrel-roof is modelled on reed roofing of mud-brick sanctuaries dating from prehistoric times. The structure here shown is symbolic and factitious and has no real inner volume.

Above right:
A cobra freize crowns the wall of the main courtyard of Zoser's temple. Beneath this sculptured crowning, redans culminate in a design characterized by lintels surmounting stone cylinders meant to simulate the roller-blinds used for closing doorways.

ing limestone and granite blocks. Actually, Egypt, poor in metals, has never really utilised steel. She has made little use of iron, and employed only a limited number of bronze tools. In the Old Kingdom, the implements of day to day use were generally made of stone. And the precious metals — gold and silver — were chiefly reserved for the jewels of the aristocracy, temple ornamentation and funereal pomp.

We may therefore affirm that Egyptian civilization is but a monumental expansion of neolithic culture. The Old Kingdom is in this respect quite revealing of the Stone Age in which predynastic traditions imprison the world of the Pharaohs. Moreover, this mastery of stonework makes possible the great works of architecture so eminently characteristic of Egyptian art and thought.

The Birth of Architecture

The emergence of stone architecture is an unexpected event. It entails a genuine revolution in Egyptian technology. This contribution is due to the first Pharaoh of the Third Dynasty, the great Zoser (c. 2800 B.C.) and his brilliant minister and councilor Imhotep who later on will be deified for his accomplishments in the architectural, medical, philosophical and scriptural spheres and worshipped as the patron of healers and scribes.

Previously, the Pharaohs of Dyn. I and II had built their vast tombs at Saqqara and Abydos entirely of crude brick. They erected massive oblong blocks relatively low in comparison with their length and width (exceeding at times 187 × 85 feet (57 × 26 m). As a rule, the fore-parts of these funerary structures, known as mastabas, were adorned with redans.

Fluting, alternating projections and recesses and imitation doors copy the walls enclosing the city of the living, in the fertile plain.

Imhotep, who erects for Zoser a grandiose funerary complex on the fringe of the desert at Saqqara, bequeaths to Egyptian architecture a series of fundamental technical solutions and a consummate and imposing decorative language. His first attempt is a master stroke. To be sure, the use of stone is not introduced without previous, preparatory trials:

16

Left :
At Dahshur, south of Saqqara, the Pharaoh Seneferu, first ruler of the Fourth Dynasty and father of Cheops, built about 2700 B.C. the so-called "Rhomboidal Pyramid". The conspicuous lower angle of its upper half explains the name given it.

Detail of the "pyramid texts", graven about 2430 B.C. on the walls of the burial chamber of Unas, a Pharaoh of Dyn. V. This is the oldest surviving important religious text.

Bird's eye view of the great pyramids of Giza: in the foreground Chephren, the summit of which is still adorned with its original outer coating, and on the right, the great Cheops. In the background, the Nile Valley.

limestone and granite floorings, facings and flaggings were tentatively employed in Dyn. II. The innovation brought about by Zoser's monument is a general "petrification" of all structures previously carried out in brick, wood or thatch. The aim is to ensure perfection and eternal duration. The quest for eternity is a constant preoccupation and source of anxiety for the ancient Egyptians who sought to enshrine the eternal gods worthy of imperishable temples.

For Pharaoh's tomb, stone replaces crude brick masonry and the all too frail wooden wainscot and door panels.

Imhotep's second contribution is the invention of the pyramid. Superimposing four mastabas of decreasing dimensions, he erects on the ruler's tomb a steplike structure symbolizing the heavenward ascension of the deceased according to Heliopolitan solar doctrines. In the final stage of construction, he adds two more steps and increases the pyramid's volume on two sides. The finished monument reaches a height of 198 feet (60 m), rising up from a nearly square base 394 feet (120 m) long and 361 feet (110 m) wide. The six stages tower above the vast rectangular enclosure formed by a wall with redans 33 feet (10 m) high and 5420 feet (1650 m) round, i.e. 1805 × 903 feet (550 × 275 m).

This gigantic monument includes, under the pyramid itself, a maze of galleries and vaults hollowed out of rock 98 feet (30 m) beneath the surface of the plateau, with burial chambers entirely lined with blue faïence tiles and low reliefs depicting the king taking part in ritual celebrations. In addition, we discover a series of subordinate structures : an entrance colonnade, a square enclosed by the famous cobra wall, rows of chapels lining a courtyard, various shrines and the Northern and Southern Houses, all examples of solid stonework with here and there barrel-roofs recalling the reed roofing employed by the common people. The most striking aspect of this symbolic but factitious architecture is the subtlety of its forms. Immediately its symmetry is apparent ; its artistic expression sure. The columns — always recessed and built into the adjacent walls with either concave or convex fluting foretell Greek solutions. Elsewhere we find trompe-l'œil ornamental features : false doors, false log rafters, dummy roller-blinds, imitation wooden railings, half-open doors with "petrified" hinges and sockets, etc. At the first attempt height is perfectly achieved. The material employed is a gorgeous fine limestone cut in regular blocks of every increasing dimensions. The first small blocks are but an imitation of former brickwork. Later on stonecutters will realize that it is more economic to work with

The Sphinx of Chephren, sculptured about 2650 B.C., stands out against the pyramid of Cheops at Giza. This enormous statue topping the body of a lion with the head of the Pharaoh Chephren himself keeps watch over the necropolis.

The columnar hall in Chephren's Valley Chapel. The unadorned simplicity of the mortuary temple and the tremendous granite blocks used in its construction (weighing over ten tons each and transported all the way from Aswan — 620 miles [1000 km] to the south) bear witness to the extraordinary mastery of architecture already attained in the Old Kingdom.

large blocks until finally in the Fourth Dynasty, we meet with cyclopean granite blocks weighing at times over ten tons.

After Zoser, the rulers of Dyn. III can but strive to equal Imhotep's grandiose constructions. Their endeavors fail however and no new advances are made before the next dynasty, when Cheops, Chephren and Mycerinus conceive of geometrically regular pyramids with triangular faces, such as those we see at Giza, among the most renowned of all mankind's creations. The period of the pyramid-builders is ushered in by the two pyramids of Dahshur, in the reign of Pharaoh Seneferu : the northern one forms a perfect pyramid reaching a height of 345 feet (105 m) on a base 729 feet (222 m) square ; the southern one, known as the "Rhomboidal Pyramid" because of the visible lower angle of its upper half, is also nearly 328 feet (100 m) high. Its base is 617 feet (188 m) square and it contains, strangely enough, two superimposed burial-chambers, the symoblic meaning of which has yet to be satisfactorily explained.

The Pyramids of Giza

Nothing can adequately describe the awe that all travelers feel at the sight of these three great pyramids, their "inhuman" mass, their proportions far surpassing our faculty of perceiving : Cheops, built in 2650 B.C., is the largest known structure in human history. This stupendous heap of limestone blocks, each one weighing 3-4 tons and occupying a volume of 71 cubic feet (nearly two cubic metres), measures, at its base, 755 feet (230 m) on all sides and 481 feet (147 m) from the base to the summit ; its area exceeds five hectares. The sum total of the materials employed amounts to a volume of one hundred and six million cubic feet (2 ¹/₂ million cubic metres) and a mass of six million tons. These colossal blocks were moved without the help of wheeled vehicles, solely

The copper-skinned general and high priest of Heliopolis, Rahotep, casts his keen and sparkling eyes in the direction of the hereafter.

Above left:
With its cristal encrusted eyes and perfectly preserved polychrome ornamentation, the statue of Nofret, found in the mastaba of her husband Rahotep at Meidum, dates from the beginning of Dyn. IV. This forty-seven century old masterpiece manifests the intense vitality of Old Kingdom sculpture.

The main chapel in the sepulchre of Mereruka, vizier of the Pharaoh Teti. This mastaba was built at Saqqara about 2400 B.C. In the columnar hall, the minister's statue, sheltered in a niche, receives the offerings of priests entrusted with the funerary cult.

Below left:
A series of tombs cut out in the rock-face of the cliff overlooking the valley across from the modern city of Aswan, bears witness to the antiquity of this site formerly regarded as the gate of the inundation. During the Middle Kingdom, rock-tombs replace in this region the mastabas peculiar to Lower Egypt. The use of rock-tombs becomes general at Thebes during the New Kingdom.

on sledges pushed along inclined planes : wet mud functioning as a sort of "skating rink" on which the flat faces of the blocks slid quite easily. We should not forget that the pyramids' sides were originally arrayed with a smooth and glossy facing setting forth the symbolic meaning of the triangle, believed to represent the sun's rays converging to a point and thus forming a "Jacob's ladder" joining earth and heaven.

In addition to the enormous pyramid with its galleries and burial rooms, its vaults and treasure chambers — plundered in ancient times — there are the subordinate structures, also worthy of note : the high temple, erected at the foot of the "artificial mountain", and the low temple in the valley — both built of cyclopean blocks of Aswan granite — are joined by a 1641 feet (500 m) long, once covered, cyclopean Causeway.

Is this work of overwhelming proportions the mere fancy of a megalomaniac ? This explanation — widely held from Pharaonic times up to the present day — seems a bit simplistic. The pyramids were more likely the fruit of a collective enterprise, intended to give the entire population a share in the resurrection of the monarch-god. This association was founded on what we might call a "guaranteed employment" system ahead of its time. Indeed, the land as well as the crops belonged almost exclusively to the Pharaoh who stored the grain and distributed it in time of famine. A powerful central government sought to minimise the speculations of certain great feudal land-owners (whose influence steadily increases in the following dynasties). In return for the livelihood thus assured them during the months when the low water level put a stop to all tillage of the parched soil, the valley's inhabitants directed their efforts to the great task of aiming to preserve cosmic order and call down heaven's blessings on the land of Egypt.

Only such a part played in the nation's salvation can explain the perfection and splendour of the monuments conceived by the rulers of Dyn. IV, 4600 years ago. Undoubtedly the best testimony to the concern of the god king's subjects for their own salvation is found in the shelter they sought for their tombs in the shadow of the colossal mountain, as if to take advantage of its beneficent presence.

The Middle Kingdom and its Unique and Precious Objects

After the glorious blossoming of the Old Kingdom, the monarchy grows steadily weaker and power falls into the hands of the provincial lords whose authority and succession becomes hereditary. A genuine feudal system is thus created. The heads of the provinces, or nomes, no longer pay tribute to the central treasury. The ruler is powerless and social order threatens to collapse.

The impending revolution breaks out in 2280. At one point Pharaoh himself falls into the hands of the rebel bands. His palace is plundered. The pyramids and royal tombs are desecrated. The treasures hidden in their secret chambers are dispersed along with the remains of the god-kings.

Wealth changes hands and "the country whirls round like a potter's wheel". Anarchy reaches a peak in this land formerly so well ruled by a supreme authority, which co-ordinated the agrarian land arrangements and irrigation in the face of recurrent flooding. This state of utter chaos will continue until the year 2065. For two long centuries Egypt loses her might, her influence, her creativity, and sinks into a maelstrom of confusion.

Once the crisis has passed, local political entities gradually re-establish their authority over the provinces. The princes of cities far

While the most outstanding examples of Old Kingdom art are to be found in Lower Egypt, in the environs of Memphis, we also encounter funerary monuments in other regions. At Aswan, nearly a thousand kilometres farther south, various princes of the Old and Middle Kingdom hollowed out rock-tombs in the bluff overlooking the Nile. In one of these tombs we may see this beautiful limestone low relief. It depicts one of the provincial lords, holding a mace, seated on a chair the legs of which have the shape of lion's paws.

View from the summit of the cliff of Deir el-Bahri at Thebes. The ruins of Mentuhotep I's funerary temple commemorate the reign of the first king of the Eleventh Dynasty and founder of the Middle Kingdom, about 2000 B.C. This terraced temple with its peristyle surrounding a pyramid now destroyed, also included a sanctuary hollowed out in the rock. It marks the beginnings of the importance of Thebes as capital of the reunified realm. Later on, the rulers of the Middle Kingdom return to Lower Egypt and found a new capital at Lisht near the Fayyum.

The White Chapel at Karnak, the only Middle Kingdom monument that has been entirely preserved, was erected under Sesostris I, second king of the Twelfth Dynasty, about 1950 B.C. The chapel or shrine of the sacred bark was discovered dismantled in the Third Pylon of the temple of Amun. This edifice, object of an exemplary anastylosis, work of the French Egyptologist Chevrier, is one of the gems of Karnak.

removed from the ancient capital — such as Aswan and Beni Hasan — restore a semblance of social order. They lay claim to the prerogatives formerly belonging to the Memphite Pharaohs. This provincial aristocracy is a source of revival, opening the way for the Egyptian renaissance.

Unity Restored

The subsequent reunification of this land, deeply shaken by two hundred years of anarchy, is the achievement of a man born not in Memphis, in Lower Egypt, but in Upper Egypt. His name is Mentuhotep I (2050) and he is destined to transform the humble market-town of Thebes into a national metropolis.

He erects his funerary temple crowned by a pyramid perpetuating Old Kingdom symbolism, at the foot of the cliffs of Deir el-Bahri. This dynamic dynast is not lacking in subtlety: the works of architecture left by him — though now in a state of utter ruin — bear witness to his remarkable sense of grandeur and proportion. His temple, with its inclined planes, terraces, peristyles and the chapel carved out of the cliff, prepares the ground for another monument equally admirable and built for posterity. We speak of that erected by Senenmut for Queen Hatshepsut six centuries, later, a hundred metres farther north, designed according to the same principle of terraces, ramps and colonnades.

In the Twelfth Dynasty, about 1990, Egypt recovers all her might during the reigns of Ammenemes and Sesostris. These two kings establish their capital at Lisht near the Fayyum, on the dividing line between Lower and Middle Egypt. This region goes through a period of extraordinary development due to gigantic irrigation works. Everything seems to have been brought back to its former state: the Pharaohs raise pyramids and colossal funerary temples and the central government is firmly re-established.

Sesostris I, surmounted with his royal cartouche, offers incense to the god Min, depicted as the cosmic generator. This champlevé low relief graven on a wall of the White Chapel along with exquisite hieroglyphic inscriptions well proves the high quality of Middle Kingdom architecture.

Fine limestone pillars seen in the shrine of the sacred bark erected by Sesostris I at Karnak: Egyptian sculptors created a most imposing décor.

23

This army of bronze Phenician gods, discovered in the foundations of the Obelisk Temple at Byblos (Lebanon), dates from the 19th century B.C., when the Egyptians established their control over the ports on the east coast of the Mediterranean. The kings of Byblos became the vassals of the Pharaohs of the Middle Kingdom.

A Dearth of Monuments

Alas! almost no significant architectural relic of this glorious era remains. The famous Labyrinth (vast funerary temple of Ammenemes III), admired by the ancients as the Pharaohs' most remarkable creation, has been entirely destroyed, as were the pyramids of Lisht, often built with a dirt and gravel filling underlaying a stone facing which was salvaged and re-used by later quarriers.

However, by a stroke of luck, archaeologists have discovered all the constituent parts of a small construction dating from the Middle Kingdom : several dozen disjoined blocks of fine limestone, delicately carved, incorporated in the foundations of the Third Pylon at Karnak, raised by Amenophis III. Carefully removed, studied with regard to their ornamentation and inscriptions, reassembled like the pieces of a puzzle, these blocks have produced one of the most beautiful anastyloses known to Egyptology : the White Chapel or shrine of the sacred bark, built by Sesostris I, about 1950 B.C., now rises up intact, pure and resplendent.

The structure's unadorned classicism, stripped of all that is unessential, as well as its champlevé low reliefs depicting the ruler offering a sacrifice to the god Amun whom we see here symbolized as Min, the cosmic generator, bears witness to the quality of architectural trends prevailing in the Middle Kingdom. While the most interesting feature of this masterpiece is its harmonious simplicity, we should not forget that it is the only Middle Kingdom construction that has been entirely preserved. If we are to believe the chroniclers, the creations of this three century long period were on the whole extremely sumptuous and ostentatious.

Left:
The Obelisk Temple at Byblos reveals the influence exerted by Pharaonic sun-worship and in particular by Heliopolitan traditions on the Phenician cult. An immense treasure was found in this sanctuary, characterized by its towering forest of monoliths.

In order to ensure the supply of cedar — necessary for the construction of a fleet of seafaring ships, as well as for the framework of palaces — the Egyptians extended their dominion all the way to the mountains of Lebanon.

Navigation and Eastward Expansion

The Middle Kingdom also renews the foreign policy of the Memphite Pharaohs. Egypt carries on an intense trade with the coast-town of Byblos.

Is Byblos an Egyptian colony?

The possibility should not be ruled out. In any case, we can be sure that close commercial relations, based largely on Egypt's need of cedar, bound this port to the Delta.

Business intercourse with the Phenician coast was first established by the Thinite kings in the fourth millenium B.C. A discovery made in 1954 bears witness to the already considerable extent of such trade during the reign of Cheops, about 2650. Two sea-faring vessels, entirely dismantled but intact, were found at the foot of the great pyramid where they had lain for four and a half milleniums on the bottom of a pit hewn out of living rock of Giza and covered over with forty-one protective limestone slabs.

These boats which have revolutionized our hypotheses concerning Egyptian navigation, are made of cedar. What do we know of shipbuilding in Pharaonic Egypt? Almost nothing, apart from what we have learned from certain low reliefs such as those adorning the tomb of Ti at Saqqara, where we can see the final stages of one such construction. For this very reason, the discovery made at Giza is of great importance. It has revealed the existence of enormous vessels capable of braving the high seas. It has made known to us the methods used by Egyptian naval architects. A patient labour of reassembly has enabled us to reconstruct one of these vessels : it is 121 feet (37 m) long! Certain wooden beams, 12" (30 cm) thick, reach a length of 75 feet (23 m) and weigh two tons. This boat is truly built on the scale of the great pyramid of Cheops!

The mode of construction was somewhat surprising : indeed, we find neither keel nor frame, contrary to what we had thought to be a formula in use since ancient times. The planks are assembled by means of a system of holes gouged in the wood and running through the timbers, in lieu of nails or rivets. These holes form curved passageways opening inwards at both ends. Strong ropes fastened the planks together.

In fact the ship was entwined and woven like a basket. Easy to disassemble, it was also flexible and perfectly watertight. The more the hull was saturated with water, the more the planks swelled up and strained the ropes, making the seams all the faster. Thus there was no need of calking, veneering and varnishing.

A vessel of these dimensions also proved the great importance of trade with Lebanon, since its construction required tons and tons of wood imported from the mountains overlooking the Phenician coast.

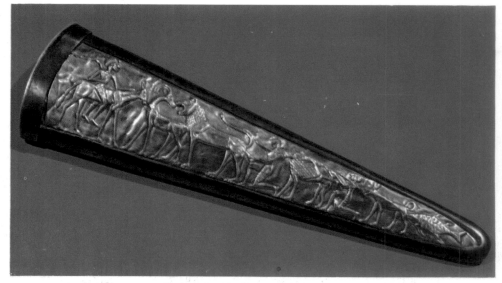

Phenician ceremonial axe found at Byblos. On the handle we see delicate granulated ornament. The gold blade offers characteristic oval apertures.

Left :
The tiara crowning this gilded bronze statuette found at Byblos reveals an unquestionable Egyptian influence. It is indeed quite similar to the crown of Upper Egypt. The same figure is depicted in profile on the handle of the gold dagger (above left).

Facing page :
This magnificent gold dagger discovered at Byblos dates from the 19th century B.C. On the handle we see butting goats, emblem of Mesopotamia. Lions, ibices, hounds, cynocephalous apes and a horseman riding bare-back make up a lively frieze on the chased gold scabbard.

Byblos, an Egyptian Trading Station

Beginning with Ernest Renan in 1860, followed by Pierre Montet in 1920, archaeologists have occupied and excavated the promontory of Byblos — or Gublu, the Assyrian Gebal. Expeditions under the direction of Maurice Dunand have brought to light a multitude of cities built one on top of another in the course of five milleniums.

In 3000 B.C. temples and an enclosure wall mark this Phenician trade port, already a port of call for the vessels of the Pharaohs of the Old Kingdom. A new place of worship is raised on the ruins of a temple destroyed by the Amorites in the twentieth century B.C. Adorned with crude obelisks — the "masseboths" doomed to abomination by the Bible! — this sanctuary bears witness to the influence of Egyptian religious doctrines. These monoliths raised up towards the sun have a good deal in common with the granite needles erected by Sesostris I at Heliopolis.

Egyptian influence is strongly marked at Byblos, the Pharaohs exert a strict control over the port and its governer-king. The reason is quite simple : for centuries already, the sole task of Middle Eastern merchant fleets has been to export cedar — the primary cause of Phenicia's commercial development — to the Nile Valley. The evergreens of Mount Lebanon furnish the entire Middle East, so poor in trees, with building materials destined to form the framework of ships and palaces. In the Middle Kingdom, this dependency increases until Byblos becomes an Egyptian vassalage.

Several objects displaying typically Egyptian workmanship were discovered in the royal sepulchre of Abi-Shemu, king of Byblos who ruled about the same time as Ammenemes III (1850 B.C.). Their presence here proves the authority exercised over Phenicia by the kings of the Nile Valley. This chased gold diadem is adorned with keys of life, djed *pillars and the insigne of power. It is surmounted with a bronze cobra inlaid with gold, representing the god of Buto, patron of Lower Egypt.*

In the Obelisk Temple built in the 19th century B.C., Maurice Dunand brought to light countless offerings giving us an idea of Phenician art and religion. These gifts to the gods make up an authentic treasure. Among other things, we find marvelous emblematic axes made of gold or electrum, typical of the style of Byblos, with oval apertures in the blades. Bronze statuettes of the god Baal. A dagger proving the virtuosity and eclecticism of Phenician goldsmiths. The gold scabbard displays a syncretic iconography : lions and ibices native of the Iranian steppe, fish and hounds from the land of the Amorites, Egyptian cynocephalous apes next to a horseman riding bare-back, foretelling as it were the Hyksos hordes whose vanguard has perhaps already appeared on the confines. On the dagger's golden handle, the butting goats of Sumer and Babylon alternate with the characteristic silhouette of the rulers of Byblos, wearing a tiara recalling the crown of Upper Egypt.

In the royal tombs, however, authentically Egyptian relics come to light. The ancient kings of Byblos lay buried in the shadow of a Gothic

This polychrome glass pectoral set in gold bears the double effigy of Ammenemes III wearing the crown of Upper Egypt. Between the two portraits of the Pharaoh, we see the falcon Horus spreading his wings. This jewel was also found in the tomb of the Phenician king Abi-Shemu.

Left :
Small blue glass bust doubtless made in Egypt. It too was found in a royal tomb at Byblos.

Far left :
Small obsidian unguent jar with gold leaf rims : this example of Egyptian craftsmanship is characterized by the austerity typical of the Middle Kingdom.

This Egyptian solid gold pectoral with openwork design, bearing the cartouche of Ammenemes III, was discovered in the tomb of Abi-Shemu at Byblos. The jewel is decorated with a series of magical signs intended to protect its owner : cobras, two udjat eyes and the symbols of the cow-goddess Hathor, the Egyptian ruler's nurse.

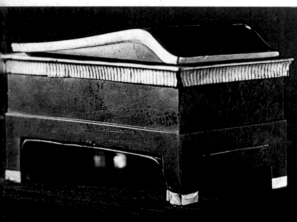

This gold and obsidian casket with its ribbed lid modelled on sanctuaries in the southern part of the Nile Valley is one of the examples of Egyptian workmanship found in the royal sepulchres at Byblos dating from the 19th century B.C.

Above:
The sneering-faced, grotesque god Bes was a familiar spirit of the Egyptians who often made magical amulets bearing his effigy, as for example this ivory statuette found at Byblos.

fortress built by the Crusaders. Archaeologists have unearthed, intact, enormous stone sarcophagi, hidden in deep hypogea carved out of the rock under the city of the living, sheltering the remains of the Phenician monarchs of the 19th century B.C. They were buried under their palace overlooking the shore. Their discoverers were quite surprised to find, in the tombs of Abi-Shemu and Ip-Shemu-Abi, proof of far-reaching relations with the rulers of the Middle Kingdom. Diadems topped by the Pharaonic uraeus, obsidian urns bearing the name of the mighty Ammenemes III, caskets with hieroglyphic inscriptions, exquisitely wrought gold pectorals — all undoubtedly the work of Egyptian artists living about 1850 B.C.

During this epoch, the two civilizations were so closely united that Phenician scribes, before inventing their own alphabet — which we ourselves are destined to inherit — quite readily read and wrote Egyptian hieroglyphics. Moreover, Egyptian was spoken at the courts of the Phenician and Palestinian dynasts.

Maritime Commerce

These Egypto-Phenician relations give us an idea of what the Mediterranean Orient may have looked like forty centuries ago, dotted with ships equipped with square sails and oars, carrying their heavy cargoes of precious building materials and exotic goods, or coasting from the Delta to Syria via the ports of Gaza, Ascalon, Tyre, Sidon, Biblos and Ugarit. We can also imagine the expeditions launched on the Red Sea in search of spices and perfumes, all the way to the Arabian and Abyssinian coasts...

To better conjure up these great journeys, we may consult the numerous models or miniatures — such as those discovered in the tomb of the vizier Meket-Rē, minister of Mentuhotep, at Deir el-Bahri, representing a veritable squadron. This flotilla, very accurately copied in wood and cloth, is composed of cruisers, cargo-ships, fishing-boats, an armed convoy-ship, etc. It proves that the part played by navigation in Egyptian life was not limited to the burial rites — with the barks of the deceased, intended to carry souls on their journey in the afterworld. On the contrary, the fleet was an indispensable tool of Pharaonic imperialism.

Detail of a Middle Kingdom hieroglyphic inscription graven in limestone.

Countless models of boats have been found in Egyptian tombs. They bear witness to the great importance of commercial navigation on the Nile and the Mediterranean as well as to religious doctrines according to which a frail skiff was supposed to carry the soul on its journey through the lower heavens. This vessel equipped with a square sail was discovered in the tomb of the vizier Meket-Rē at Deir el-Bahri. It dates from the Eleventh Dynasty, i.e. about 2000 B.C.

Detail of a vessel found in the tomb of Meket-Rē : we see here the canvas-covered arched cabin. Under the supervision of a boatswain, sailors raise the yard supporting the sail.

COLLEGE LIBRARY
COLLEGE OF TECHNOLOGY
CARNARVON ROAD
SOUTHEND-ON-SEA. ESSEX

Like the White Chapel, this pavilion erected by Amenophis I in 1550 B.C. was discovered dismantled in a pylon of the temple of Karnak. The austere perfection displayed by this edifice dating from the beginning of the New Kingdom and the finely carved alabaster blocks used in its construction recall the creations of the Middle Kingdom.

From the very beginning, the New Kingdom manifests a trend towards continuity: Queen Hatshepsut's mortuary temple, built at the foot of the cliff of Deir el-Bahri opposite Thebes, about 1500 B.C. The architect, Senenmut, drew inspiration from the near by temple of Mentuhotep I. The edifice built in terraces lined with double porticoes stressing the horizontal, forms a striking contrast with the vertical faces of the cliff.

The New Kingdom : the Dominance of Thebes

At the end of the reign of Ammenemes IV (1790), Egyptian ascendancy in Asia abruptly collapses. Anarchy sweeps the country. The cause of this disorder is not clear. In 1730, the Hyksos, attracted by the impotence of a state enfeebled by internal dissension, push their way into the Delta — which, up to that time, had been generally safe from invasions, an island protected by desert flanks on the east and on the west.

Actually, migratory movements cause repercussions in the entire Near East : Indo-Aryan hordes successively invade the region and jostle the ancient civilizations. The Hittites occupy Cappadocia, the Hurrians reach the Euphrates, and the Kassites take possession of Mesopotamia.

Façade of the chapel of Anubis in the north wing of Queen Hatshepsut's temple at Deir el-Bahri. One should take note of the elegant so-called "proto-Doric" columns with their sixteen-sided shafts topped with an abacus by way of capital. They furnish us with an example of Egyptian classicism, ten centuries before the dawn of Greek civilization.

The Hyksos Invasion

The Hyksos invaders — given by Menatho the name of "Shepherd kings" on account of their nomadic origins — gradually infiltrate the eastern part of the Delta. About 1700, they are in power in Lower Egypt. They establish their capital at Avaris, otherwise known as Tanis.

The main cause of their military success — they progressively take possession of the whole of Egypt — is the use of horses and chariots, previously unknown in the region. These regiments on wheels completely change land strategy, formerly based on infantry manœuvres alone. Swift chariot attacks render the battles lopsided. Even in relatively small numbers, their mobile contingents rout the Egyptians who will in turn be obliged to employ the new weapon.

After 150 years of foreign occupation, Thebes gives the signal for casting out the Asiatic barbarians. The Pharaoh Amosis I (c. 1590) takes Avaris and puts an end to Hyksos domination.

A Quick Revival

From this time forward, Thebes replaces Memphis as the capital of Egypt, from both a political and a religious standpoint. The great temple of Amun, "king of the gods", is built at Karnak. Opposite it, on the "bank of the dead", the Pharaohs of the Eighteenth, Nineteenth and Twentieth Dynasties will erect their funerary temples and lay out their tombs in the Valley of the Kings.

As after the great revolution that put an end to the Old Kingdom, the reunification marks the beginning of a new era in Egyptian glory. Once more, the Pharaohs renew the traditions of their great past. From the very beginning, the New Kingdom is characterized by a firm will to revive the traditions of the Middle Kingdom.

Hathoric capital bearing the effigy of
Queen Hatshepsut portrayed as the goddess Hathor — in the south wing of the
temple at Deir el-Bahri.

Detail of a proto-Doric column in
Hatshepsut's temple: the gorgeous fine
limestone used in construction well becomes
the severe simplicity of this order. The
austere and unadorned capital is crowned
with a pure Egyptian cavetto cornice.

Right:
View of the rock amphitheatre of Deir el-
Bahri with the Kurn overlooking the valley. In the foreground, Queen Hatshepsut's mortuary temple with its two terraces
joined by ramps. In the background, the
sole terrace of Mentuhotep I's temple, built
during the Middle Kingdom; it manifestly
inspired the architect Senenmut, the
queen's confidant and favourite.

A good example of this continuity is the pavilion built by Amenophis I, son of Amosis, about 1550 B.C., in the temple of Karnak. Found disassembled in the foundations of the Third Pylon (along with the White Chapel of Sesostris I), this small structure built entirely of alabaster has been reassembled stone by stone. It is now nearly intact and gives us an idea of the very classic purity of line in vogue at the dawn of the New Kingdom. Its delicately engraved panels framed with tori (a type of molding borrowed from pisé architecture) and crowned with the typical Egyptian cavetto cornice, make this shrine of the sacred bark a masterpiece of simplicity.

During the reign of Tuthmosis I, who succeeds Amenophis I, the country experiences a period of great territorial conquests, reestablishing the Pharaoh's ascendancy both in Asia, where his armies cross the Euphrates, and in Nubia, where Egyptian troops reach the Fourth Cataract, nearly 620 miles (1000 km) south of Thebes. The greatest era of Egypt has begun. It continues under Tuthmosis II, first husband of Queen Hatshepsut.

The Reign of Queen Hatshepsut

The only woman to rule over Egypt (before the Ptolemies and the famous Cleopatra), Hatshepsut, daughter of Tuthmosis I, took in marriage her half-brother, as was the custom at the Pharaohs' court. The death of her husband gives the dynamic queen a free hand. She contracts a second marriage with her own brother, Tuthmosis III, in order to legitimate her rule while maintaining her new husband in the humiliating situation of a "prince consort". This capable woman who proclaimed herself king, usurped royal titles and wore the false beard as a badge of her authority, raised a sanctuary modeled after Mentuhotep's funerary temple and conceived by her architect and favourite, Senenmut.

Hatshepsut's funerary temple at Deir el-Bahri represents unquestionably one of the most fascinating successes in Egyptian architecture. The problems solved well prove the architect's talent, though he essentially followed Mentuhotep's example. Like its model dating from the Middle Kingdom, the queen's sanctuary is spread out over a distance of 1 km. Starting in the cultivated fields of the valley, a causeway lined with sacred trees slopes gently upwards to inclined ramps flanked by colonnades supporting terraces. At the ramp's end, the temple runs up against the mountain and plunges into the 394 feet (120 m) high cliff locking the rock amphitheatre surmounted by the Kurn, a natural pyramid overlooking Thebes.

Thus built at the foot of the Libyan mountains, the temple, spread out over 328 feet (100 m), appears quite striking in its harsh, rocky setting.

Proto-Doric columns in the chapel of
Anubis in the north wing of Hatshepsut's
temple. Remnants of polychrome ornamentation may still be seen on the low reliefs
adorning the walls.

Queen Hatshepsut's soldiers celebrate their
home-coming after an expedition to the
land of Punt in the Red Sea in search of
spices and perfumes. Low relief in the
chapel of Hathor in the temple at Deir el-
Bahri.

The cliff is used as a background, setting off the monument. Senenmut, faced with the task of incorporating his creation into this mighty vertical rampart as a harmonious element of the landscape, decides to stress the horizontal. His temple is composed of relatively low porticoes spread out over 181 feet (55 m). The supports composing these porticoes are simple square pillars with neither base nor capital, laid out in front of each of the two lower terraces. Eleven pillars stand on the left and on the right of the ramp. The third tier is composed of an equal number of supports. Here, the pillars are adorned with Osiride statues bearing the effigy of the queen. They form the vestibule of a hypostyle hall followed by the holy of holies with a vaulted ceiling hewn out of rock.

On the northern side, we see the famous "proto-Doric" columns. They characterize both the side portico and the small chapel of Anubis. These sixteen-sided columns — from a distance they appear to be fluted — are topped with a simple abacus, by way of capital. The shafts, made up of drums piled one on top of another with neither entasis nor batter, are set upon round, flat bases. The airiness and delicacy of this order which seems to foretell classic Greek architecture a thousand years ahead of time, forms a contrast with the prolixity and gigantism of Ramesside creations. Indeed, Senenmut's art, as we see it at Deir el-Bahri, touches us chiefly by its proportions, always kept on a human scale.

In this temple, the queen commemorates the outstanding events of her reign. The low reliefs adorning the porticoes depict in particular an expedition made by sea to the land of Punt, in all likelihood none other than far-off Ethiopia or Southern Arabia. Egyptian sailors brought back incense, myrrh and precious aromatics to be used for embalming, as well as ivory and highly-prized wood.

Tuthmosis, Builder of Empire

When the reign of the female Pharaoh comes to an end, Tuthmosis III takes his revenge on the author of his humiliation; he gives the order to erase all the cartouches bearing Hatshepsut's name, as well as all the portraits adorning her temple. Tuthmosis III, empire-builder, shows out to be a redoubtable conquerer whose annual campaigns in the Near East silence the turbulent Syrian princes, always ready to shake off the Egyptian yoke. He consolidates Egypt's position on the upper Nile and takes Meroe, on the Fourth Cataract.

The empire is now firmly established, wealth and tribute flow into Thebes where the temple of Amun occupies a more and more important place in the political arena. Under Amenophis II and Tuthmosis IV, Egypt enters into an alliance with Mitanni. The Pharaohs wed Mitannian princesses, thus ratifying their military treaty.

The reign of Amenophis III is a period of peace and prosperity for Egypt (c. 1400 B.C.). The ruler devotes his energies to the construction of a gigantic funerary temple. Two enormous colossi bearing his effigy guard the entrance. These monolithic statues later on become a custom. This phenomenon probably indicates a change in the mode of worshipping the god-king. It will result in stupendous technical strokes of skill. Thus each of the two seated colossi of Amenophis III — now better known as the colossi of Memnon — is sculpted in a block of quartzite no less than 49 feet (15 m) high, not counting the pedestal. These blocks weigh some 550 tons. They were brought over a distance of 435 miles (700 km) from the eastern desert near Aswan.

As for the temple itself, it was built on the same scale: pylons and hypostyle halls now entirely destroyed rose up in an enclosure 1969 feet (600 m) long from front to back. The monument, ravaged by an earthquake, was apparently used as a quarry no later than the Nineteenth Dynasty, i.e. less than a century after its construction. Its architect, the prince and royal scribe Amenhotep, son of Hapu, nonetheless remained famous and, like his great predecessor Imhotep, was even deified.

The Colossi of Memnon erected in front of Amenophis III's funerary temple, built about 1400 B.C. The temple, soon destroyed by an earthquake, was used as a quarry as far back as the Nineteenth Dynasty. The gigantic seated statues of the Pharaoh, mutilated but restored during the Roman period, now stand alone amidst fields submerged by the flood waters of the Nile.

Egypt and Death : the World of the Necropoleis

The great problem for the Egyptians was death. It was their major preoccupation, their sole concern, realising, as they did, that their everyday environment, constructed in perishable materials, would disappear. The only remaining witnesses of the Egyptian race are their temples and necropoleis. For the inhabitants of the Nile Valley, the belief in life after death is perfectly obvious. The deceased must therefore be accompanied on his journey to the afterworld by everything that delighted him here on earth : food, drink, furniture, riches, etc.

But, above all, his body must not perish. Hence the idea of mummifying and embalming corpses. Mere internment in desert sands dried up the flesh and partially preserved the features of the deceased. This natural process was combined with aromatic and natron treatments. The viscera and the brain were removed so as not to corrupt the rest of the body. A method of "packaging" using cloth wrappings was perfected. Sarcophagi became stronger and more airtight. All of this contributed to the survival of the body destined to resuscitate.

We have already mentioned the efforts made by the dynasts of the Old Kingdom to preserve their remains in enormous funerary edifices (mastabas and pyramids). But the king is not the only person who seeks eternity beyond death. The tombs of the nobles soon cluster up around Pharaoh's. These tombs are veritable abodes hollowed out of the rocky plateau, complete with chapels, peristyles, treasure chambers and corridors, grouped within massive mastabas. Like the dwellings of the liv-

These three charming young musicians make up one of the most famous compositions in New Kingdom painting. They may be seen in the tomb of Nakht in the necropolis of Kurna at Thebes. Nakht, a scribe in the temple of Amun, lived about 1425 B.C. Apparently, he wanted music to resound not only at his funeral feast but also during his life in the netherworld.

Like a pyramid, the Kurn overlooks the Valley of the Kings. The royal hypogea of the New Kingdom were hollowed out in this universe of rock and death. Only one of them escaped the greed of grave-robbers : the tomb of Tutankhamen, the entry of which may be seen in the foreground on the right.

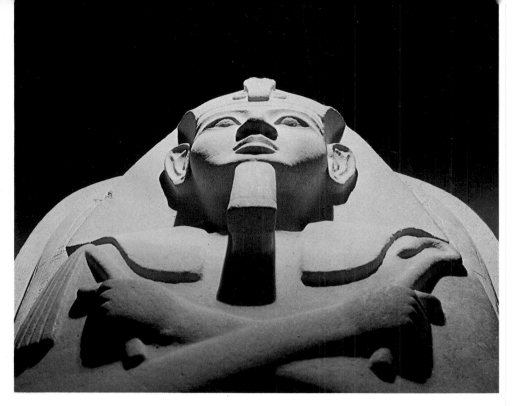

The granite sarcophagus of Ramesses IV in his tomb in the Valley of the Kings. The ruler's effigy, armed with the whip and sceptre, has slept for over 3000 years in his desecrated sepulchre in the heart of the sacred mountain.

Chamber in the hypogeum of Queen Nofretari, wife of Ramesses II, in the Valley of the Queens: in the centre, the queen, wearing the loose pleated linen robe characteristic of the New Kingdom, is guided by the goddess Isis, portrayed in the traditional Egyptian sheath dress. The goddess reassures the queen and leads her before the scarab-headed god symbolizing the rising sun and the resurection of the flesh.

ing, these funerary structures are disposed along streets and avenues where the priests, entrusted with the task of assuring the next life of the dead, bustle about their business.

Though pyramids are still built in the Middle Kingdom, we also find, in the region of Beni Hasan, tombs cut out of the cliffs that hem in the valley. These tombs contain the first Egyptian "proto-Doric" columns. A similar type of rock-tomb may also be seen at Aswan, sheltering the remains of the governers of the province. This is the form preferred by the nobles of the New Kingdom. When the seat of government is moved to Thebes, genuine underground cities for the use of the aristocracy are carved out of the cliffs west of Luxor and Karnak. The nobles take advantage of the economic boom resulting from Pharaonic imperialism, to erect splendid sepulchres.

These hypogea are carved out of soft limestone crossed by veins of chalk and kidney-shaped gravel. The walls are plastered. On these walls painters execute vast compositions uniting subjects illustrating the life of the future occupant of the tomb and symbolic figures by way of provisions for his journey to the afterworld. In addition to classic scenes depicting the tomb's owner sailing a papyrus skiff in the marshes, hunting game birds with a boomerang or fishing with a javelin, we also find representations of agricultural labour (plowing, sowing, reaping, grape-gathering), feasts complete with musicians and dancers, or also funerals with their weepers and the cortège of the tribute-bearers These paintings give us information about day to day life : we see the nobles at work and at play, among other more stereotyped images taken from the funerary texts (magic tables, psychostases, patron deities, etc.).

As for the Theban Pharaohs themselves, the systematic plundering of the pyramids in times of troubles has made them wiser. In the New Kingdom, they separate the two main aspects of internment : the funeral ceremony takes place in the temple built on the west bank, whereas the burial itself is now accomplished in a tomb destined to remain unseen.

Goddess adorning the tomb of Horemheb : Isis crowned with the sun's disk.

Left :
A scene of country life in the tomb of Menna, at Kurna near Thebes. This work dates from 1400 B.C. After the harvest, oxen tread out corn on the threshing floor.

Above left :
The tomb of the Pharaoh-general Horemheb, responsible for the restoration of orthodoxy after the religious crisis that took place during the reign of Akhenaten, about 1340. It is one of the most beautiful sepulchres in the Valley of the Kings. Colourful wall paintings, characterized by bold outlines and vivid contrasts, are splendidly preserved : here we see the goddess Hathor, patroness of the necropolis, granting the Pharaoh her protection.

Far left :
The entire ornamentation of Tuthmosis III's tomb is copied after a papyrus of the Book of the Dead, with its lively sketches portraying fearsome monsters.

41

An almost modern simplicity of line characterizes this stellar divinity, haunting the rock-tomb of Tuthmosis III.

Above right :
This small pyramid crowns a New Kingdom tomb at Deir el-Medina. The sepulchre in question contains the remains of a workman employed in the Theban necropolis.

The workmen's village now known as Deir el-Medina lies in a narrow gorge between the fertile valley and the mountain overlooking the Valley of the Kings. This site has yielded priceless information on the teams of craftsmen who decorated the sepulchres of the nobles, kings and queens of the New Kingdom.

These tombs are hidden in the barren waste land of the Valley of the Kings, at the foot of the Kurn, the shape of which recalls a natural pyramid overlooking Thebes. A syrinx, i.e. a narrow gallery cuts into the mountain to a depth of ten or more metres (or even 361 feet [110] in the case of the hypogeum of Ramesses VI !). The entry was concealed by a cone of fallen earth and debris in order to save the tomb from the greed of grave-robbers, all too well informed of the immense treasures buried along with the ruler's remains.

Some sixty tombs have been identified within the confines of the Valley of the Kings, shielded against the raids of desert plunderers by walls barring the more accessible passes. All had been profaned and ransacked, except for the tomb of Tutankhamen. Most of them present an extraordinary spectacle meant to fulfill a magical purpose and guide the deceased through the ambushes and dangers abounding in the hereafter, haunted by monsters and dreadful spirits. This painted ornamentation, often very colourful, illustrates the famous funerary texts of the Book of the Dead, or Book of What There Is in Hades, or Book of Gates, also known as the Writ of the Hidden Chamber, incantations intended to

break evil spells and grant the deceased eternal life. Hence these gods who give judgment, these boats in which the deceased sails, these ordeals undergone by Pharaoh, victorious and triumphant, the gods' equal. The reliefs displaying the mysteries of the netherworld still remained to adorn the walls of the long galleries and desecrated tombs.

The royal brides also had their Valley of the Queens, on the other side of the mountain. Some of these tombs, such as that of Nofretari wife of Ramesses II, are among the most beautiful and the best preserved we know of.

What moles burrowed out the titanic Theban necropolis? We find the answer to this question in the workmen's village at Deir el-Medina. Built at the foot of the bluff lodging the New Kingdom rock-tombs, the walled village has yielded up heaps of precious information, sketches on potsherds (ostraca), minutes of proceedings instituted against robbers, petitions, accounts of strikes made by poorly paid workers, etc. We learn how work was done in shifts. We catch a glimpse of the existence of these marvelously talented artists who gave life to the dazzling message of Egyptian painting.

On the very bottom of the Valley of the Kings, the tomb of Tuthmosis III presents an ornamentation that differs considerably from that of other royal hypogea: an enlarged copy of a funerary papyrus, the Writ of the Hidden Chamber. This extremely simplified drawing depicts a bark of the dead sailing in the afterworld.

Painted stucco portrait of the mystical Pharaoh Akhenaten, prophet of the Aten, considered as sole god and symbolized by the sun's disk. This work dating from about 1360 was discovered at Tell el-Amarna. It reveals the intense spirituality of the Pharaoh intoxicated with divinity (Staatliche Museum, Berlin).

This painting on plaster, originally adorning a palace in Tell el-Amarna, depicts, with the familiarity typical of the Amarna fashion, two of the daughters of Akhenaten and Queen Nefertiti. The elongated head, sunken chest and wide hips are characteristic of the new style in vogue during the heretic period (Ashmolean Museum, Oxford).

The Great Religious Crisis: from Akhenaten to Tutankhamen

During Amenophis III's reign, the thousand year old Egyptian religion undergoes certain transformations touching in particular the cult of the Pharaoh. As it appears, the imperialist system entailed a certain syncretism of Egyptian and Middle Eastern cults, the outcome of which was a manifest need for a unified religion capable of crowning both the Nile Valley polytheism with its countless deities and the growing monotheistic aspirations of Egypt's possessions in Palestine, Phenicia and Syria. Previously, the Heliopolitan cosmology prevailing in Lower Egypt and centred round Rē, had been given as a counterpart in Upper Egypt the god Amun of Thebes, who thus became the great Amun-Rē of the New Kingdom. This king of the gods, including and preceding them

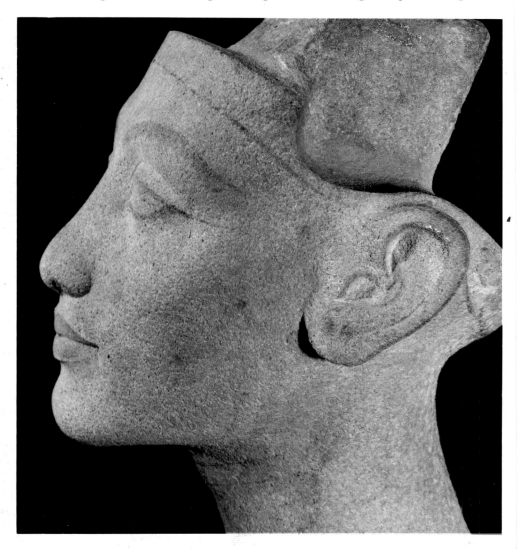

Perfect symbol of the feminine ideal, this profile of the beautiful Nefertiti, brought to light in the studio of the sculptor Dhutmose at Tell el-Amarna, is one of the masterpieces of Pharaonic art. It is a mere unfinished study: the high head-dress widening out at the top, dear to the queen, is lacking.

Unguent box in the shape of a royal cartouche. It belonged to Tutankhamen. These receptacles, covered with chased gold leaf plating and adorned with polychrome glass inlays, furnish us with an image of the youthful king, bearing the insignia of power.

Right :
This solid gold mask set off with polychrome enamel inlays, covered the face of Tutankhamen's mummy. The Pharaoh died in 1345 B.C. According to an Egyptian text, "gold is the indestructible flesh of the gods". This mask is one of the most perfect masterpieces of Pharaonic art.

all, has his temple at Karnak, henceforth the most important sanctuary in the country.

This vast trend towards religious unity and the worship of one sole god testifies to a spiritual uneasiness, a quest. Under Amenophis III, about 1400, theological speculations attempt to consolidate the great god's supremacy by means of various appelations : the Unique, the Hidden One, the Unknowable One, i.e. the Aten, embodied by the Sun's Disk. The Valley's polytheism, resulting from the conjunction of diverse ethnic groups, seems about to be transformed into a monotheistic system. The son of Amenophis III — first known as Amenophis IV, a name which he later changes for that of Akhenaten — repudiates Amun-Rē and proclaims the Aten the unique and supreme god of the empire.

The all-mighty Pharaoh, prompted by an irrepressible mystic enthusiasm, regarding himself as the Aten's first prophet, thus undertakes a strange religious revolution. By virtue of the power conferred on him as absolute monarch, he decides on a reform intended to democratize the cult : henceforth the gloomy temples, esoteric realm of the priesthood, closed to the faithful, are replaced by a cult of the sun, worshipped in the light of day and open to all comers. Egypt was ill prepared for such an upheaval. She was asked to abolish all of a sudden all her time-honoured beliefs and worship the visible sun alone, whose theologist-prophet was none other than the ruler, Akhenaten, aided by his wife, the beautiful Nefertiti.

Akhenaten, who reigns from 1372 to 1354, desires above all to break away from Theban influence. He brings the priests of Amun to heel and founds a new capital in Middle Egypt : Akhetaten, the modern Tell el-Amarna, complete with temples, palaces, diplomatic archives, a river port and rock-tombs. The mystic adventure of the royal couple, intoxicated with the new divinity, will be enacted on this site.

The Amarna fashion in art is characterized by a will to abandon the stiff hieratism of the cult of Amun-Rē in favour of a more straightforward, vivid and familiar portrayal of ordinary life, representing man in society as well as in relation to his maker. Amarna art is an expressionist art. While the portraits of the beautiful Nefertiti found in the sculptor Dhutmose's atelier attain an acme of grace and idealization of feminine features, on the other hand the colossi of Karnak, enormous "caricatures" portraying the ruler himself, bear witness to a trend wholly foreign to ancient Egyptian art.

The Atenist reign is a dramatic interlude that lasts only sixteen years but exerts an unquestionable influence on Egypt's spiritual and artistic evolution. The rulers' pacifism also has disastrous consequences on an international scale. The Pharoah's subjects and satellite states, aware that their attempts to regain independence will meet with but a feeble opposition, progressively break away from the empire.

Akhenaten and Nefertiti have six daughters but no male offspring. The king therefore marries one of the princesses to prince Tutankhaten, whom he has chosen as his successor. Tutankhaten, last son of Amenophis III and Queen Tiye, is but ten or eleven years old when the heretic Pharaoh dies. He is better known as Tutankhamen.

Akhenaten had no sooner died than a foreseeable reaction set in. The cult of the Aten is abolished, the city of Akhetaten razed to the ground, Amun-Rē's cult re-established at Karnak. The young Tutankhamen is given a coregent, but the edict putting an end to the heresy is signed by the child-Pharaoh himself. This colourless person dies after nine years of rule, in 1345, before the age of twenty. He was the last member of Dyn. XVIII.

A Fabulous Treasure

This unknown adolescent king, mere tool of the orthodox reaction, is destined, paradoxically enough, to have an incredible posthu-

Gilded wood effigy of the goddess Sekhmet, portrayed as a lioness, destroyer of the Sun's enemies. This sculpture is part of Tutankhamen's treasure. The goddess, crowned with the sun's disk, is wearing the traditional narrow sheath dress. Her wide hips recall the Amarna fashion.

Above right:
Polychrome alabaster unguent jar decorated with hunting scenes and topped with a feline bearing Tutankhamen's cartouche. This work, executed in a rather bland style, was probably used in the ritual embalming of the Pharaoh.

mous fame. The whims of fate will spotlight this brief and inglorious reign, the reason being that Tutankhamen's tomb is the only royal sepulchre in the Valley of the Kings discovered intact by archaeologists.

About sixty years ago, the English Egyptologist Howard Carter decided to explore systematically the Valley of the Kings, in search of the tomb of Tutankhamen, a Pharaoh almost unknown even among specialists. His expedition, financed by the Earl of Carnarvon, set to work in 1919. In 1921 the venture seemed hopeless and Carter's grant was about to expire when the expedition, discouraged, decided — flying in the face of facts, since the syrinxes were generally cut out of the cliff walls — to study the bottom of the valley, beneath the entrance to Ramesses VI's hypogeum. On November 4, 1922 Carter discovered steps making up a stair-case carved in the rock. These steps led to a sealed door, behind which he was to find the most fabulous treasure mankind had ever dreamt of.

The task of extricating, preserving, consolidating and transporting the several thousand objects contained in this tomb where no man had set foot for 3250 years required a decade of patient labour. An attempted robbery made shortly after the interment had thrown the sepulchre's contents into utter confusion. It was however discovered quite quickly by the guardians of the Valley of the Kings who hastily walled up the small hypogeum. Apart from this insignificant incursion, the sepulchre and its incredible treasures were found untouched.

Archaeologists were dazzled by these treasures: statues, couches, chairs, chariots, caskets and jewels, to say nothing of the mummy's extraordinary solid gold mask contained in a solid gold coffin followed by two more gilt coffins and a stone sarcophagus, protected in turn by four nested gilt shrines, providing an everlasting shelter for the deceased monarch's corpse.

Gilded wood statue portraying Horus, the falcon-headed sun god. This work, found in Tutankhamen's tomb, proves the restoration of Theban orthodoxy.

Back of Tutankhamen's royal throne: a very lavish scene adorns this work in gold-plated wood set off with glass and enamel inlays and semi-precious stones. Under the sun's disk depicted in the new style (rays are shown with hands), the king, in a graceful reclining pose, is waited upon by the young queen Ankhesnamen. On the right, on a wooden stand, we see a gold and jewelled necklace similar to those worn by the monarchs.

Statuette in the shape of a divine mummy meant to represent Tutankhamen. Such statuettes, known as Ushabti figures, were regarded as substitutes for the deceased. This wooden figurine covered with gold leaf is adorned with black and dark blue features indicating the eyes and false beard.

The treasures brought to light in Tutankhamen's tomb are particularly interesting as unquestionable examples of the art then in vogue at the emperor's court. This is obvious, judging from the many exotic materials employed and the countless subjects of inspiration. The art in question is showy and ostentatious, seeming at times even somewhat characteristic of a parvenu.

The Amarna Fashion

However these works also illustrate the distinctive character of the Amarna fashion and the religious concerns of an epoch obsessed with intense mystical yearnings, as if the Amarna crisis had been but the result of Egyptian opulence.

As if metaphysical anguish could be given an artistic outlet solely in a world safe from material anxieties. In short, as if the Aten drama were but a luxury indulged in by a civilization that had already reached the peak of wealth and power.

The perfection of these works of art overwhelms us. In particular the solid gold funerary mask with its enamel inlays is a genuine technical achievement : in the age of handicrafts, we see here a creation that, to say nothing of its aesthetic qualities, attains the perfection of a machine-finished precision work. Gold metallurgy is so well mastered that the artist's personnal imprint is well nigh imperceptible. This gold mask represents as it were a symbol of material perfection, brought to life by the spiritual tension that alone can account for the absolute mastery of an art.

A similar perfection is characteristic of the pieces of furniture with their haughty or exquisite "modernism", and the polychrome statues. Inlays ornamenting the back of the gold throne portray the royal couple's family life. Queen Ankhesnamen, depicted in a graceful and relaxed pose, anoints her royal spouse, Tutankhamen, with perfumes. Hunting scenes, the style of which foretells the great low relief of Medinet Habu, show us the Pharaoh in his chariot, holding a bow.

In short, this post-Amarna art with its ostentation, delicacy and occasional prolixity, as well as the bland affectation of its alabaster works, marks a dividing line between Akhenaten's familiarity and Ramesses II's majestic hieraticism. It is a touching example of the protean versatility displayed by "immutable Pharaonic art".

Utter confusion in which Howard Carter found Tutankhamen's tomb in 1922. On the left, overturned chariots and, on the right, ceremonial couches in the shape of imaginary animals occupy the antechamber of the royal sepulchre.

Facing page :
On his journey through the netherworld, foretold by the funeral ceremonies, Tutankhamen was supposed to be changed into the god Anubis, lord of the necropolis, portrayed as a black dog. This important wooden statue is adorned with gold inlays and alabaster and obsidian eyes.

Ushabti *figure of Tutankhamen equipped with a cane crowned with the emblem of the* djed *pillar and the key of life. The king, wrapped in protective wings, is wearing a wide necklace and a quite unusual spherical helmet.*

This painted wooden head portrays Tutankhamen as a child: the elongated skull recalls the Amarna fashion. An exaggerated liveliness is characteristic of all works produced during the reign of the heretic king.

This odd polychrome alabaster bark with its baroque cabin in which we see a young lady with her dwarfish slave, is one of the "ornamental" objects, the baffling style of which forms a striking contrast with the majority of the works of art found in Tutankhamen's tomb.

The Orthodox Reaction

Nevertheless, after the religious crisis and the brief interregnum characterized by the triumph of the orthodox reaction, the Egyptian throne remains vacant. The country has lost its colonial empire. A general, Ay, former loyal supporter of the Aten and preceptor of Nefertiti, returns to Theban orthodoxy and assumes the reins of government. Another general, Horemheb, succeeds him and expunges the names of his two predecessors from the royal Canon. Two viziers who help him to restore the empire, Ramesses and his son Sethos, found the Nineteenth Dynasty which will lead Egypt to the pinnacle of glory.

Tutankhamen as harpooner. The king, wearing the crown of Lower Egypt (the hunt took place in the marshes of the Delta), is standing up in a papyrus skiff. This 30" (75 cm) high gilt statue represents the mythical combat between the god Horus and his brother Seth.

This lion's head, similar to those adorning the gold throne, is carved at the head of Tutankhamen's ceremonial couch.

Ramesses II, the Power and the Glory

The outer courtyard of the temple of Luxor was built by Ramesses II in front of the monumental colonnade that Horemheb usurped from Tutankhamen. Between the sandstone columns, Ramesses II raised granite colossi bearing his own effigy.

When the young Pharaoh Ramesses II comes to the throne of Egypt in 1301 B.C. at the age of twenty, he inherits a mighty empire restored by warlike kings — the great general Horemheb, followed by Ramesses I and Sethos I — after Akhenaten's disastrous foreign policy of non-intervention and straightforward unconcern.

Ramesses II, who has ruled jointly with his father, Sethos I, is well aware that the main danger to peace lies on Egypt's northern boundaries. The Syrian and Palestinian possessions reconquered by his father remain under the Hittite threat. This Anatolian tribe is following a policy of expansion by all possible means: treaties, infiltration and revolts fomented on the confines of the Egyptian empire.

Sethos I had already been obliged to give battle under the walls of the stronghold of Kadesh, veritable bastion lying on the bank of the Orontes, not far from the Lake of Homs in Syria (less than 6 miles [10 km] from the northern border of present-day Lebanon). In this first encounter, the Hittites had been defeated and their king Muwattalis had withdrawn his troops and signed a peace treaty with Egypt. But the Hittite monarch, to whose name the Egyptians henceforth add the appellation of "the fallen one of Khatti", does by no means consider himself vanquished. He is planning to take his revenge.

New Capitals

The festivities that greet Ramesses' accession to the throne quite naturally imply a loosening up of Egyptian control. The garrisons of the Syro-Palestinian fortresses are faced with constant revolts. Kadesh has been abandoned to the Hittites. Ramesses II, aware of the peril hanging over his empire, wishes to move his headquarters closer to the zone of operations: he leaves the remote religious capital, Thebes, in Upper Egypt, and founds on the eastern fringe of the Delta a wholly new politico-military capital which he names Pi-Ramesses. This splendid stronghold probably rose up on the site of Tanis (formerly Avaris). Ramesses is thus in a position to counter the scheming of his redoutable Hittite adversary.

Muwattalis executes a similar manœuvre: he temporarily transfers his capital from Khattusas, situated in the very heart of the Anatolian plateau, to the ancient city of Kanesh, farther south beyond the Halys river.

Thus these two all out enemies prepare for the great clash of empires that shall decide the fate of the two great powers of the thirteenth century B.C.

Granite colossus of Ramesses II. Ramesses, who ruled over Egypt for 67 years, from 1301 to 1235, led a life full of wars and gigantic architectural undertakings advertising his own glory.

A bay in the great Hypostyle Hall at Karnak, the construction of which was begun by Amenophis III and Sethos I and completed by Ramesses II. This immense hall 172 feet (53 m) from side to side and 335 feet (102 m) from front to back, includes 134 enormous columns and rises up to a height of 79 feet (24 m).

Overleaf:
The romantic ruins of the Ramesseum, funerary temple of Ramesses II, erected at Thebes on the west bank, at the foot of the Kurn. The enclosure wall was destroyed by the Assyrians; the hypostyle halls now stand out in the full light of day. In the centre, the second courtyard, lined with Osiride colossi bearing the monarch's effigy.

The Adversaries

The antagonism can be no greater: Ramesses II who has inherited a thousand year old empire, has the ardour and self-reliance of youth. Muwattalis, already in the twentieth year of his reign, governs a recently created empire. He is endowed with experience, craft and a good knowledge of tactics.

Faced with an impending revolt in Palestine, Ramesses II, in the fifth year of his reign, assembles his forces: professional soldiers forming a unified and well co-ordinated army. He dresses four divisions of some 9000 men each. This army of over 35,000 men, with their chariots and baggage train, rushes across the Sinai desert, leaves behind the cities of Gaza and Megiddo and finally reaches the border and the banks of the Orontes.

Muwattalis, on his own account, has called together his Syrian and Mittanian vassals, raising troops in northern and western Anatolia. In the region of Aleppo, he will be joined by the allied forces of the land of Amor. The Hittite army comprises 3500 chariots, each one drawn by two horses and carrying three warriors (a driver, a shield-bearer and a lancer-archer), all in all more than 10,000 men reinforced by two bodies of foot-soldiers, one of 8000, the other of 9000 men. As we see, the forces mustered by the two opponents are more or less equal.

The Ambush

The swiftly advancing Egyptian troops string out in the forests of Lebanon. The four divisions (bearing the names of Rē, Amun, Ptah and Seth) move fearlessly forward. Self-styled deserters paid by Muwattalis have informed Pharaoh that the enemy is still in the region of Aleppo, far to the north. The unsuspecting Egyptians encamp in sight of Kadesh, which they hope to reconquer. They make ready to besiege the stronghold and carry it by assault, believing it shelters but a small garrison.

Hittite war chariot as portrayed in a low relief found in Carchemish. The driver and archer occupy a two-wheeled vehicle drawn by only one horse adorned with a crest. On the ground, an enemy soldier is trampled under foot.

Facing page:
This important low relief decorating the Ramesseum depicts the battle of Kadesh where, in 1296 B.C., the troops of Ramesses II faced the Hittite army led by Muwatallis. The Pharaoh, who miraculously escaped from the Hittite encirclement and managed to break free from the vice in which Muwattalis had caught him, here lays claim to victory. The indescribable rough-and-tumble of warriors and chariots vaguely recalls the lively and straightforward Amarna fashion, here applied to a typical battle scene in favour with the warlike kings of the Nineteenth Dynasty.

Hittite soldiers, hurled into the Orontes, swim across the river in order to join the bulk of their army, massed on the other bank. Detail of the low relief depicting the battle of Kadesh.

The capture of the city of Dapur by the troops of Ramesses II. This low relief decorates the first hypostyle hall in the Ramesseum. Dapur was a Syro-Palestinian stronghold the Egyptians took by assault in 1290 B.C. after having besieged it with engines of war such as ladders, climbing irons and broad shields employed for forming testudos intended to protect the besieging troops from the enemy's arrows. The vanquished jump from the summit of the fortifications or try to flee by means of ropes while the arrows of Pharaoh's archers shower upon them from all sides.

Facing page:
Low relief adorning the Ramesseum. Ramesses II, victorious, still wearing his battle helmet, reports to the great god Amun of Thebes and prepares to receive the whip and battle-axe, symbols of his power.

In the meantime, Muwattalis, having lulled the 25 year old Pharaoh into security, manœuvres in order to take his enemy by surprise and attack his flank. However, an Egyptian liaison squadron has at last managed to take a few prisoners who are brought before Pharaoh and questioned. It becomes clear that the main body of the Hittite army is not far off. Before the Egyptians can muster their forces, the first waves of Hittite chariots unfurl on the camp, sowing panic among the unwary Egyptians.

Ramesses II has no choice but to jump into his chariot. Muwattalis, however, has executed an outflanking movement, cutting the monarch off from his troops. In any case, the two remaining Egyptian divisions are still far off and their leaders do not know that the battle has been engaged.

Ramesses Breaks Free

Two thousand five hundred Hittite chariots attack the divisions of Amun and Rē, under Pharaoh's command. The Hittites rush the Egyptian camp before their enemy can organize his defense. Almost alone, deserted by his troops, Ramesses, attempting to break loose, hurls his chariot against the ranks of the foe. His valour and spirit work a miracle. After several desperate attempts, he manages to get free of the vice in which Muwattalis had caught him. Luckily, the treasures in which his camp abounds have dazzled the Hittites. Busy pilfering all they can lay their hands on, they neglect to consolidate their victory and grant their enemy a respite that proves fatal.

After hour long heroic combats, the Egyptian divisions receive reinforcements: these fresh troops rush into the thick of the fray and push back the Hittite army. Muwattalis falls back upon Kadesh. But the Egyptian army has suffered great losses. Ramesses can no longer consider besieging a well armed enemy. Though part of the Hittite troops have been drowned in the river, Muwattalis has still over 1000 chariots held in reserve.

All Sides Victorious

In short, the two opponents, realizing that their forces are equal, avoid a decisive battle. Once back in their capitals, both celebrate their victory. Ramesses' exploits are glorified in one of the longest texts in Egyptian literature, the poem of Pentaur. The author of this admirable epopoeia employs "a technique half-way between Homer and our own heroic

At the foot of the colossal statues of Ramesses II at Abu Simbel, we find the graceful effigies of Queen Nofretari. These Nubian temples, lying 217 miles (350 km) south of Aswan, have been the object of an extraordinary rescue operation that required the entire disassembly of the sanctuaries, the cliff in which they were sculptured being cut into blocks. The temple of Abu Simbel now rises up anew in its former beauty and majesty on the water's edge, 230 feet (70 m) above its previous emplacement, submerged beneath the waters of the Aswan High Dam.

poems''. Pharaoh who feels himself lost, alone amidst his enemies, cries unto the gods and pathetically begs their assistance. Amun answers the king's prayer, granting him the courage and strength necessary to break free and join his troops. This text exalting the valour of the Egyptian ruler is not however the only monument raised to commemorate the battle of Kadesh, well nigh fatal to the Ramesside prince. In the many temples built during his 67 year reign, Ramesses II continually immortalizes this "victory" by means of inscriptions and low reliefs. Actually, the "victory" consists in the mere fact of having avoided a disastrous defeat and captivity. But official communiqués are not troubled by such subtleties. Thanks to this tremendous encounter, Egypt will be enriched with new works of art, far more vivid than all that has come before. The sense of movement, keen observation and violent, startling short cuts we see here were perhaps favoured by the new perception of nature resulting from the Amarna reform...

Although extolled and portrayed on the walls of the Ramesseum, "King Usimarē's Mansion of Millions of Years", funerary temple of Ramesses II, christened "Osymandyas's Tomb" by the Greek historian Diodorus who deformed the ruler's prenomen; although carved at Abu Simbel in the great speos, now rebuilt out of the reach of Lake Nasser's waters, this "victory of Kadesh" does by no means entail a withdrawal of the Hittite threat. On the contrary, Kadesh remains in the hands of Muwattalis, as well as the entire land of Amor.

The Hittite king has not given up his expansionist designs. He soon foments a new revolt in Palestine. But he dies while Ramesses once again sends off his troops to curb the insurrection. During this second campaign, the Egyptians take the stronghold of Dapur, south of Aleppo (1290). This victory is also portrayed in low reliefs on a wall of the Ramesseum.

Peace Re-established

Khattusilis III who succeeds Muwattalis after a period of disorder in Anatolia, makes offers of peace. He invites Egyptian plenipotentiaries to negotiate in his capital Khattusas, now Boghazköy, a tremendous stronghold enclosed by a wall 3.7 miles (6 km) round, complete with a vaulted underground postern giving the besieged the possibility to slip behind the impressing glacis protecting temples and palaces and attack the enemy in the rear.

The treaty signed by Ramesses II and Khattusilis III in 1280 is the first great international agreement the text of which has been preserved. It establishes an Egypto-Hittite condominium in the Middle East. Thirteen years later, this accord between the two former enemies is still intact and Ramesses ratifies the peace treaty, taking for wife one of Khattusilis's daughters. This political marriage is celebrated at Pi-Ramesses in the 34th year of Pharaoh's reign. No longer occupied on his north-eastern borders thus rendered safe from attack, Ramesses is now free to devote all his energy to the great architectural performance that shall characterize his reign.

Colossal Achievements

The fact is that Ramesses, who rules to the age of 87 and has over a hundred "Royal Children", literally covers Egypt with monuments, from the Delta to Upper Nubia. His chief architectural creations are the Ramesseum, the great Hypostyle Hall at Karnak, the colonnade of Luxor and the speos of Abu Simbel. But we must also mention the tremendous granite colossi, monoliths bearing his effigy and weighing up to a thousand tons, carried on rafts from Aswan all the way to Thebes and

The great speos of Ramesses II at Abu Simbel as seen before the rescue operation. We should notice the colossi carved in the sandstone cliff. Each of these gigantic portraits of the Pharaoh is almost 82 feet (25 m) high. The four statues — one of which collapsed centuries ago — stand out against the cliff, in the same position in which they might have been raised in front of the pylon of a temple built in the plain. They are arranged by pairs on either side of the entry to the speos.

The small speos of Abu Simbel, dedicated by Ramesses II to his wife Nofretari. The façade offers six standing statues, no more than 33 feet (10 m) high, chiselled in the rock of the cliff. The king's wife is portrayed as the beautiful goddess Hathor.

Memphis. We must neither forget the border fortresses, the new cities such as Pi-Ramesses, the "House of Ramesses Great-of-Victories", nor Pi-Tum, near the modern Suez Canal.

Nonetheless, the most spectacular work of this glorious reign in which everything is done on a colossal scale, is undoubtedly the great temple of Abu Simbel, fronted by four seated "portraits" of the ruler, nearly 82 feet (25 m) high, carved out of the cliff, greeting the rising sun. Behind this majestic entrance, the edifice plunges into the rock where we find a first hall adorned with Osiride pillars also bearing the monarch's effigy and a second hall preceding the holy of holies, not forgetting a series of side chapels, vestry-rooms and depositories for sacred objects.

This structure lying 217 miles (350 km) south of Aswan was threatened with submersion in 1965 when the waters of the High Dam started to rise. A rescue operation undertaken with the cooperation of UNESCO and a group of specialists, engineers and qualified workmen from the world over, succeeded in preventing the irreparable loss of the 3200 year old masterpiece.

In order to save all the sculpted surfaces of the façade and underground sanctuaries, the rock face was scalped and the cliff cut up into over a thousand blocks weighing twenty or thirty tons each. The temples have now been re-erected 230 feet (70 m) above their previous emplacement : the disassembled blocks have been carefully put back in place, the speos re-created with an invisible cement skeleton, the rock setting reconstructed on all sides. The constructions of Ramesses II have been carefully replaced in their former position facing the rising sun, the god Rē to whom this prodigious sacred sculpture is dedicated.

We see here, dismantled, the three colossal heads of Abu Simbel. The colossi of Ramesses II thus decapitated in 1966, were reassembled in 1967, when the temple recovered its ancient splendour 230 feet (70 m) above its original emplacement.

The rescuing of Abu Simbel, threatened by the rising waters, was so urgent that work went on night and day.

Above left:
Osiride pillars representing Ramesses II support the ceiling of the main hall in the great temple at Abu Simbel, entirely hewn out of rock.

We find the same gigantic proportions in the famous Hypostyle Hall at Karnak with its 134 columns. The highest ones, lining the central bay, support heavy stone lintels rising up, at their highest point, 79 feet (24 m) above the pavement. This volume 328 feet (100 m) from side to side and 164 feet (50 m) from front to back was considered already in ancient times as one of the Wonders of the World, visited by Greek and Roman travelers. The author of these extraordinary creations, Ramesses II, prompted by a genuine "building fever", quite literally studded Egypt with monuments.

Far left:
The rescue operation destined to save the great speos of Abu Simbel in 1965: sand bags protect the temple's monolithic façade which will later be cut into blocks weighing several tons each. These blocks are then conveyed to a storage area where they await reassembly.

This monumental gatehouse modelled after those of Syro-Palestinian fortresses leads into Ramesses III's funerary temple, built at Medinet Habu across from Thebes, about 1180 B.C. Its broad windows and strictly vertical walls have no counterpart in Egyptian architecture.

The temple of Medinet Habu, seen from the shore of the sacred lake. The enclosure wall, the monotony of which is broken by two great pylons, is almost intact.

The "Sea-Peoples" and Ramesses III

Lengthy reigns are almost always a cause of disorder, the government's authority necessarily declining when the ruler becomes senile. Thus, in the Old Kingdom, the era of revolutions begins under Pepi II, who lives to be a hundred and governs for eighty years (the longest reign in history !). The final result is total chaos. In the last years of Ramesses II's reign, though to a lesser degree, Egypt also meets with increasing difficulties : the old Pharaoh who remains on the throne to the age of eighty-seven, formerly held the country in an iron grip. In his declining years, he loosens his hold and grants himself a respite which certain subdued lands do not hesitate to take advantage of. At the same time, Assyrian power is waxing and has gained a foot-hold on the Euphrates.

The most impending threat, however, lies in the north. This peril has been given a name : the "Sea-peoples", an Egyptian term covering various Indo-Aryan peoples such as the southward moving Achaeans, who settle on the coasts of the Aegean Sea. After the downfall of Knossos and the decline of Cretan power (during the reign of Amenophis III), Mycenae builds a mighty feudal state, conquers Troy and establishes its dominion on the coasts of Asia Minor in Hittite tenure ; Hittite power is waning.

But a new wave of invaders is on the move towards the Aegean : the Dorians. They in turn occupy Greece and Asia Minor, putting the inhabitants of these regions to flight. The Achaeans and many other peoples take to sea and reach the coasts of Libya and Palestine. Henceforth these maritime migrations continually threaten the Pharoah's empire.

Merenptah, the fourth son of Ramesses II, comes to the throne in 1235, after having ruled jointly with his father. In the fifth year of his reign, a band of Libyan invaders pushes its way into the Delta. They are defeated by the Egyptian ruler after an arduous combat. Is Egypt out of danger ? In reality, the "peoples of the sea" will strike their next blows on the other side of the Delta.

In spite of maintaining a brilliant façade, Egyptian society is undergoing a process of erosion due primarily to the ascendancy of the priesthood and a gradual revival of feudalism. The colonial empire that ensured Egypt's opulence thanks to the many tributes paid to the treasury, is now lost. The country is thrown back on its national boundaries. Egypt, so long accustomed to great wealth, faces an acute economic crisis. Too many prisoners taken in Ramesses' campaigns have settled down in the valley and serve in the militia. The monarchy collapses and a series of ephemeral rulers briefly occupy the throne.

About 1200, Ramesses III restores the monarchy and firmly establishes a central executive power. He rebuilds the army and the fleet

Vestiges of the royal palace may still be seen south of Ramesses III's funerary temple. In the background, the enormous brick wall, more than a kilometre long, behind which the kings of following dynasties seek refuge from the disturbances that shake the country.

Important remnants of polychrome ornamentation subsist in places under the lintels surmounting doors in the temple of Medinet Habu. They give us an accurate idea what New Kingdom sanctuaries may have looked like in the days of their greatest glory. Here, patron vultures fly across the star-studded sky.

The portico of the second courtyard in the temple of Medinet Habu: massive square pillars support the stone slabs that make up the temple roof.

in order to cope with the ever present danger of the Sea-peoples. He defeats contingents of Libyan invaders and dispatches the bulk of his forces against Palestine and Syria. He drives the enemy back to the banks of the Orontes, thus restoring Egyptian domination in Phenicia. In the west, however, a new wave of invaders crosses the Libyan border. Once having subdued them, Pharaoh considers it politic to let them settle peacably on the fringe of the Delta, as a bulwark against further invasions.

Ramesses III thus stabilizes the situation, stimulates the economy and strengthens the army. He can now put the architects, who had been idling since the death of Ramesses II, back to work. He erects an enormous funerary temple across from Luxor at Medinet Habu. A tremendous stone gatehouse modeled after those of Syrian fortresses, gives access to the temple, surrounded by two brick enclosure walls, the outer one of which, 59 feet (18 m) high and 33 feet (10 m) thick, has a length of 1149 feet (350 m) from front to back and 3938 feet (1200 m) all round. This gatehouse commemorates Pharaoh's Asiatic campaigns. The edifice, with its broad, low windows and strictly vertical crenelled walls, is indeed a copy of the famous Asiatic "migdols" (donjons) portrayed in the low reliefs of the siege of Dapur, adorning the Ramesseum.

An ancient temple begun by Hatshepsut and finished by Tuthmosis III already existed on the same site. It was incorporated into Ramesses III's "Mansion of Millions of Years". This funerary temple is among the best preserved of all the New Kingdom sanctuaries. We can still see almost intact the two pylons preceding columnar courtyards as well as all of the outer façades characterized by high walls crowned with the classic Egyptian cavetto cornice. The hypostyle hall and the chapels surrounding the holy of holies are in ruins. South of the temple, the palace proper remains: we can recognise the harem, baths and columnar audience halls.

Beautiful low reliefs decorate the temple's walls. On the reverse side of the main pylon we see a hunting scene showing Pharaoh pursuing water buffaloes in the marshes. This picture is full of life, remarkably spontaneous in spite of Pharaoh's hieratic attitude. Indeed, we see him stiffly bending his bow while his chariot carries him forward at a gallop. Other reliefs portray a naval battle against the Sea-Peoples which probably took place in the Delta on an arm of the Nile.

Peace with the Sea-peoples is maintained after the ruler's death during the reigns of his successors, from Ramesses IV to Ramesses XI. Nevertheless, government power declines, while the priests, masters of the vast temple possessions, constantly build up their authority. The sanctuary of Amun at Karnak, for example, exerts an authority well nigh equal to that of Pharaoh himself. According to the archives, it owned and managed 240,000 hectares of fertile land.

When Ramesses XI dies, Herihor, high-priest of Amun, commander of the army and viceroy of Nubia, proclaims himself king and founds the Twenty-First Dynasty. During this period, the kingdom is divided between two rulers, one at Thebes, the other at Tanis in the Delta. For fifty years there are actually two concurrent dynasties. Times are gloomy, strikes and famine ravage the land.

About 950, Sheshank I founds the Libyan Dynasty (Dyn. XXII) and runites the country for a short time. But unrestrained anarchy gets the better of him and the decline of the Egyptian state continues; generals give the orders in both the political and religious spheres. The division into two kingdoms continues until the Cushite (Sudanese) Dynasty seizes power from Meroe all the way to the sea and governs what is now called the Ethiopian Empire, starting in 715.

But Assyrian invasions add the finishing touches to Egypt's downfall: in 671 Esarhaddon takes Memphis and in 667 Ashurbanipal conquers Thebes. In 664, after an insurrection, he sacks the city, ravages the temples, throws down the colossi and plunders the treasury.

This vast hunting scene shows Ramesses III pursuing water buffaloes in the marshes. He is backed up by an entire army of beaters and archers. This extremely lively low relief graven on the reverse side of the first pylon depicts mortally wounded animals in the throes of death while an enormous male still seeks to flee among the reeds.

Door in the temple of Medinet Habu. The typical Egyptian cavetto cornice stamped with a winged solar insignia crowns the doorway.

69

Vast paved courtyard preceding the hypostyle hall in the temple of Horus at Edfu. This enormous temple is a masterpiece of Ptolemaic architecture. Its construction required almost two centuries, from 237 to 57 B.C.

The great pylon at Edfu, 118 feet (36 m) high. On all important festivals, four deep recesses housed gigantic wooden flagstaffs carrying decorative banners.

Egypt's Swan Song: Ptolemaic Art

After six gloomy centuries of chaos, Egypt goes through a new phase of intense cultural rejuvenation during the Saite renaissance (663-341) and the Ptolemaic period. Psammetichus I throws out the Assyrians and founds the Twenty-Fourth Dynasty. His successor, Psammetichus II, subdues the Ethiopians and takes Napata.

The Saite period may be defined as a genuine cultural renaissance, characterized by vigorous activity along literary, ethical and artistic lines.

There is a will to return to the sources of the Old and Middle Kingdom, as if the newly reborn realm wished to demonstrate its attachment to its prodigious, two thousand year old past.

Saite sculpture, for example, is so similar to the great creations dating from the time of the pyramids, that modern museographers have a hard time distinguishing between the works of these two periods, separated by twenty centuries. Saite artists and monarchs seem to take an interest in archaeology: they restore temples, raise new statues executed in the ancient manner, exhume old texts and renew the cult of rulers long dead.

But they also organize daring expeditions, such as the nautical odyssey of the Pharaoh Neko (609-594), whose fleet accomplished in three years the first circumnavigation of Africa. The same monarch digs a bold and new Suez Canal and renews the expansionist foreign policy of the great reigns of the past: he re-establishes Egyptian ascendancy in Palestine and Syria but in the end is defeated by the Babylonian Nebuchadnezzar.

Detail of a granite falcon symbolizing Horus, the sun bird. He is wearing the crowns of Upper and Lower Egypt.

The temple of Edfu: view from the summit of the pylon. We see here the great hypostyle hall and the sanctuary separated from the outer wall by a ring corridor, plunged in gloom.

Palm-leaf capital in the great hypostyle hall at Edfu. One should take note of the austere elegance characteristic of this order following the time-honoured traditions of the Old Kingdom.

In the meantime, a new enemy is rising on the horizon: the Persians.

The brilliant Saite revival is cut short by the conquest of Cambyses (524). The Persians occupy the country, constantly shaken by rebellions. An insurrection led by Amyrtaeus (404) restores the independence of the Nile Valley and inaugurates a new period of liberty. In 341, the Persians return, commanded by Artaxerxes III, and once again bend the Egyptians under their yoke.

Greek Domination

The conquest of Egypt by Alexander the Great in 332 B.C. marks the beginning of an era of intense architectural activity that will continue throughout the entire Ptolemaic period. Though Egypt is now a Greek vassal and her Pharaohs foreign rulers governing in the new capital, Alexandria — as a creative centre the country's grandeur is by no means impaired.

Ptolemaic art, worthy successor of the Pharaonic world and rightful heir to Egyptian religious and architectural traditions, springs up and thrives far from the Hellenist centre and the Delta. Greek influence is little felt in Upper Egypt. On the contrary, we witness a reaction which affirms the authenticity of Egyptian thought as embodied in both sculpture and architecture. Several dozen gigantic temples erected during the six centuries preceding the ultimate collapse of the Pharaonic world attest to this flourish.

While the Greek dynasty reigns only from the 4th century B.C. to the dawn of the Christian era, Egyptian art persists in all its splendour

View of the portico lining the courtyard in the temple of Horus. The conspicuous entasis typical of columns employed in New Kingdom constructions is replaced during the Ptolemaic period by straight shafts growing somewhat narrower towards the top.

through the 4th century A.D. Edfu, Denderah, Kom Ombos, Esna and Philae, to mention but the most important and best preserved later temples, are monuments to the old civilization's intense vitality during the 650 years of Ptolemaic and Roman rule.

Efforts are made to raise anew the ruins left by the Assyrians. The aim is to rebuild the ravaged places of worship on a colossal scale, as in the days of Egypt's greatest might, founded on Pharaonic imperialism. Yet Egypt is under the heel of the Greek invader, to whom she pays tribute. The Pharaohs are foreigners who imitate the ceremonial etiquette, pomp and rituals of the Egyptian court. They have usurped Pharaonic insignia and forgotten the priests' ancient tongue. The priests alone still make use of hieroglyphic script...

Paradoxically enough, this ultimate phase of Egyptian art cannot be called decadent. Pharaonic sanctuaries rarely display an equal architectural simplicity : well defined surfaces, legible shapes and volumes, clean and uncluttered angles, all the more striking since these structures have been neither retouched nor transformed. The great religious centres of the New Kingdom, on the other hand, underwent countless modifica-

The great pylon of Edfu, seen from the corner of the portico, casts a shadow over the courtyard. This splendidly preserved twenty century old temple gives us a good idea of late Egyptian art. Only the furniture, statuary and polychrome ornamentation are lacking.

tions and complications, resulting in the colossal extensions of Karnak with its labyrinths of chambers, chapels and outlying shrines.

Added to which the desire to attain technical perfection is more conspicuous in these later creations than in the works of the Ramessides, whose building mania, aiming solely at exalting the monarch, often led to slovenliness. Architects hastily piled together heterogeneous materials and made do with unstable supports. As time goes by, the edifices suffer, the pylons fall in, the walls jut out, the foundations are swallowed up. None of this erosion occurs during the Ptolemaic period. Artists willingly devote centuries to the construction of a gigantic sanctuary. The workmen manufacture a colossal and well adjusted machine. Special care is given to the finishing touches.

The Temple of Edfu

To appreciate the great vitality of Ptolemaic architecture, so instructive, and true to the purest Pharaonic traditions of design and utilization of space, we have but to visit the great temple of Horus at Edfu. Extraordinarily well preserved, this gigantic sanctuary gives us an insight into

The façade of the first hypostyle hall at Edfu. Near their base, the columns are engaged in adjacent vaulted walls. The hall is well lighted by broad bays opening on the outside.

Between the temple's outer wall and the sanctuary proper (on the right) a ring corridor cuts the sacred zone off from the outside world. The façades, covered with low reliefs and hieroglyphic inscriptions and flanked by enormous lion-headed gargoyles, present wholly blind surfaces.

the past and discloses only the obvious aims of its architects. Indeed, the roofing and most of the ornamentation of this two thousand year old edifice have come down to us almost intact. Each room has preserved its atmosphere, just as it was conceived by its authors. Gradation is ensured by variations in light intensity catching the eye and governing our perception of space. Apart from the absence of furniture and polychromy, the temple of Edfu is the same today as in the days of its greatest splendour. The visitor fancies that the priests who quit the sanctuary 1500 years ago never again to return are going to appear all of a sudden in the half-light of a hypostyle hall, and the liturgical chants dedicated to the solar falcon will once more resound within the temple walls...

Begun in 237 B.C., the temple was completed 180 years later. This

Facing page :
Scene decorating the east end of the ring corridor at Edfu: the goddesses of the north and south crown the king, Ptolemy VI Philometor, with the red crown of Lower Egypt and the white crown of Upper Egypt. This remarkably elegant low relief was graven between 181 and 145 B.C.

The first hypostyle hall at Edfu: enormous 56 feet (17 m) high columns support the architraves of the stone roof. This vigorous architecture is by no means suggestive of a civilization near its downfall. Neither the dimensions nor the quality of the ornamentation foretell the coming cultural collapse.

Vertical view of the forest of columns composing the great hypostyle hall at Edfu. We notice the variety of composite capitals crowning the lofty shafts.

Facing page :
Deep gloom reigns in the second hypostyle hall of the temple of Horus: a few rays of light entering through apertures in the ceiling — similar to Le Corbusier's "light canons" — break the prevailing obscurity, favourable to mystery and meditation.

gigantic monument has a length of nearly 559 feet (140 m) and a width of 263 feet (80 m). The pylon rises up to a height of 118 feet (36 m), i.e. the equivalent of a modern twelve-story building. It covers an area of 75,348 square feet (7000 square metres), enclosed by a tremendous 36 feet (11 m) high wall.

The main door, situated between the pylon's two massive supports, opens on to a vast courtyard encircled by a columnar portico. The thirty-two shafts, 29 feet (9 m) high, provide a perfect setting for the lofty façade of the great hypostyle hall. Vaulted walls block the intercolumniations, except the main entrance. Supported by 18 massive colums, the hall's ceiling touches enormous lintels; the monoliths of the central aisle have a span of over 16 feet (5 m). The hypostyle hall is well lighted from the outside. Semi-darkness sets in when we reach the third bay. The hall's far end is closed by a wall characterized by a receding slope, similar to that of the pylon. In the middle of this furthermost wall is a monumental door: the third threshold we must cross before reaching the inner spaces proper. Leaving this door behind us, we find ourselves in the second hypostyle hall, immersed in a mysterious semi-obscurity. Though the columns here are not as lofty, their capitals are swallowed up in darkness. This hall, only 66 feet (20 m) long and 43 feet (13 m) wide, seems to have no visible boundaries. We have now entered into the realm of "dark night", pierced here and there by rays of light falling from apertures in the stone slabs making up the ceiling.

A fourth door, the panels of which were formerly of metal-plated wood, gives access to the vestibule, or room of offerings. Crossing the fifth and last threshold, darkness completely swallows us up, we are now in the holy of holies, enclosed within high gloomy walls, a veritable temple within the temple. A mysterious corridor into which open several chapels, runs round the sanctuary. Now everything is pitch black. A clever lighting system, calling to mind twinkling constellations, foretells the "light canons" invented by Le Corbusier.

And we arrive at last in the sparkling naos of polished black granite, work of Nectanebo II (4th century B.C.), that sheltered in times gone by the statue of the sun god, Horus, the falcon of Edfu. The priests celebrated here three daily services: at dawn, at midday and at dusk, offering the god food, sprinkling and suffusing his image with incense

Clever natural lighting near the corner of the holy of holies in the mysterious corridor of the temple of Edfu. Horizontal lighting obtained by means of loop-hole-like openings pierced near the top of the walls is here combined with vertical shafts contrived in the stone slabs composing the roof. The result is a most mystical atmosphere.

A square stair-case leading to the rooves of Edfu makes it possible to go from "the shadows of night" into brilliant sun light. A multitude of gods and goddesses accompany the priests' procession and guide them through the semi-darkness.

and exotic perfumes, delighting his ears with chants and songs. The statue was regularly washed and clothed, adorned with costly attire and jewels. Sacrificial meat, loaves and fruit were placed at its feet along with pure water drawn from the temple well.

This inspection of the best preserved sanctuary bequeathed to us by Egyptian civilization reveals several laws governing temple structure. On the one hand, the temple is a sacred, enclosed place — reserved for the god alone and his servant-priests — to which the common people are now allowed access. For this reason, the edifice resembles a sacred stronghold, complete with its defensive works. On the other hand, it was made up of multiple enclosures, housed one within another like a nest of Russian dolls. The same arrangement is used for the protective coverings surrounding the corpse of the deceased, if we interpret correctly the various layers of sarcophagi encasing Tutankhamen's mummy.

As we come closer to the sacred "tabernacle", its mystery becomes more obscure. At the same time, we notice that the height of the component structures steadily diminish. Thus we follow a gradually decreasing series from the gigantic pylon (118 feet — 36 m) to the façade of the first hypostyle hall (56 feet — 17 m), the entrance of the second hypostyle hall (39 feet — 12 m) and the vestibule (29 feet — 9 m) leading into the holy of holies (23 feet — 7 m) and the naos (13 feet — 4 m). This arrangement was already employed in the great temples of the New Kingdom, built at Thebes, on the bank of the dead, and at Karnak.

Although often disparaged by art historians who call them overwrought, Ptolemaic low reliefs are generally executed in an extremely original, purely hieratic style that has nothing to do with that of preceding epochs. In fact, the relief is more pronounced, the deities's bodies take on a certain sensuality. The sense of movement peculiar to the great military compositions and hunting scenes has vanished, giving way to a ritual immobility. The reason is quite simple : Ptolemaic art is the work of the priesthood alone and is no longer intended to glorify the king's exploits. Nonetheless its graceful silhouettes, unerring lines, delicate details, meticulously rendered jewels and attire, noble gestures and poses bear witness to the inexhaustible possibilities of stylization suggested by Pharaonic art.

Along with the countless inscriptions covering the temple's walls, columns and ceilings, the low reliefs help us to define each room's function : House of Books, Perfume Laboratory, Vestry, Shrine of the Sacred Bark, Treasure Chamber, etc. These inscriptions are commentaries on the mode of worship. The summary of the inscriptions found in the temple of Edfu alone makes up a 3000 page book. Some texts dating from this period display an admirable lyricism and depth of thought. This is particularly true of the great hymns, among the most beautiful texts in world literature.

At the far end of the holy of holies at Edfu, the gleaming polished granite naos, dating from the reign of Nectanebo, about 370 B.C. This "tabernacle", formerly concealed behind bronze or gold-plated wooden doors, contained the statue of Horus before which priests celebrated three daily services. In the foreground we see the pedestal intended to receive the bark of procession.

From Roman Domination to the Onset of Christianity

COLLEGE LIBRARY
COLLEGE OF TECHNOLOGY
CARNARVON ROAD
SOUTHEND-ON-SEA, ESSEX

The transition from Greek domination, exerted by the dynasty of the Ptolemies, to Roman supremacy is, as far as Egypt is concerned, hardly perceptible. If it hadn't been for the battles between Caesar, Cleopatra, Antony and Octavius, the event might have passed unnoticed : a mere change of dynasty, an incident of no great importance. At most, the annexation of Egypt to the Roman Empire in 30 B.C. results in the transfer of the seat of government from Alexandria to the far off metropolis of Rome.

At the same time, the country's rulers become more impersonal, more fictitious than ever before. It must be said in favour of Alexander's successors, the Ptolemies, that they at least ruled on the spot. They were still held in high esteem in the eyes of Upper Egypt's priests and sculptors. Henceforward, the Roman Emperors, who in turn usurp Pharaonic insignia in the later low reliefs, make use of Egypt's religious structure exclusively to maintain their control over the province.

They were well aware that this would be impossible if they did not yield to Egyptian traditions and play the part of the god's sovereign mediators.

These "Egyptian Pharaohs" are no more than empty, insubstantial, abstract names. To be sure, the great hymns carved on the walls of Denderah, Esna and Philae call down heaven's blessings on Trajan, Hadrian and Caracalla. This was however done exclusively to perpetuate the ancient system and maintain time-honoured forms of worship.

On the other hand, the construction of great sanctuaries continues as before. Though the Nile Valley, granary of the ancient world, is squeezed more than ever by Rome, Egyptian priests find the means necessary for erecting fantastic monuments.

While the low reliefs reveal at times certain weak points, many of them are indisputed masterpieces. While we might expect to find edifices built on a reduced scale, colossal proportions in fact persist. The great hypostyle hall at Denderah (temple built according to a plan similar to that of Edfu and, if we are to believe the inscriptions, drawing inspiration from a document dating from the reign of Cheops !), with its twenty-four sistrum-shaped columns, dedicated to the goddess Hathor, reaches a height of 56 feet (17 m). The hypostyle hall of the temple of Khonsu at Esna, built during the reign of Claudius, displays a similar gigantism with lavish inscriptions literally covering the walls, ceilings and pillars.

During the Roman period, Upper Egypt remains a busy work-yard where splendid sanctuaries continue to rise up entirely free from Roman influence.

Facing page :
The ornamentation of the mammisi (or house of divine birth) in the temple of Hathor at Denderah was executed between 100 and 140 B.C., i.e. during the reign of Trajan or perhaps Antoninus. Its character is nonetheless typically Egyptian. Delicate sculptural details, exact reproduction of apparel and vigorous reliefs endow the graceful Hathor, goddess of beauty and music, with a somewhat decadent charm.

Rescuing Philae

This marvelous art of the Graeco-Roman period has now become a focus of attraction. Long held in contempt by certain specialists, this late-blooming architecture has grown in favour with art historians, largely due to the tremendous rescue operation undertaken to preserve the temple of Isis at Philae.

Philae is a tiny granite island situated on the Nile's First Cataract above Aswan. In this grandiose wilderness (thought by the ancients to be the "flood's gate") a temple had been erected as far back as the reign of Nectanebo in the 4th century B.C. Its construction continues throughout the Ptolemaic and Roman periods. Indeed, the last hieroglyphic inscriptions adorning the temple walls are engraved under Theodosius, up to A.D. 392, when the imperial decree proscribing paganism is issued.

The temple of Philae was dedicated to the goddess Isis, symbol of fertility, and later on also of mercy, love and charity. This divinity will be an object of fervent devotion during the great regeneration undergone by the Pharaonic cults in the last days of Ancient Egypt, under the influence of religions promising salvation. We should not forget that the cult of Isis reaches Rome itself and constitutes a redoubtable threat to new-born Christianity. Hence the vitality of both the Isiac religion and the temple of Philae, the importance of which steadily increases during the last centuries of Egyptian civilization.

Quite a few constructions are crowded together on the island: in addition to the sanctuary proper, 213 feet (65 m) long, complete with its two pylons and hypostyle hall preceding a courtyard sheltering a mammisi or Chapel of Divine Birth, we also find a chapel dedicated to Osiris, a temple of Hathor, the famous pavilion of Trajan, the chapel of Imhotep, colonnades, embankments, wharves and obelisks now destroyed...

Façade of the hypostyle hall in the great temple of Hathor at Denderah. This edifice, built during the Roman period, is one of the most outstanding achievements of late Egyptian architecture. The columns are crowned with sistrum-shaped Hathoric capitals, adorned with portraits of the goddess complete with the cow-ears recalling her origin and culminating in high embellished dados.

Diagonal view of a bay in the great hypostyle hall at Denderah. The ceiling, adorned with a lavish zodiacal and astronomical iconography, bears witness to the esoteric concerns prevailing in Egypt's latter days.

The forest of massive columns in the hypostyle hall at Denderah includes a total of twenty-four shafts (as compared to only eighteen at Edfu). During the Coptic period, the portraits of Hathor adorning the capitals were defaced.

This important architectural complex was, until not long ago, submerged in a bay situated between the old Aswan Dam, built in 1899 and twice heightened, in 1907 and 1929, and the modern High Dam (Sadd el-Ali). The overfall that battered against the temple walls half-way up the pylons threatened to dislodge the sandstone blocks and erode the sculptures. For this reason, in the scope of the great rescue operations undertaken to save other Nubian temples, UNESCO studied the possibility of displacing the temple of Philae.

This task was undertaken in August, 1972. A steel sheet-pile dam 2254 feet (900 m) long was erected to isolate the submerged island from the artificial lake. The drowned temples were then pumped dry and disassembled stone by stone. Each element was given a number and the 40,000 blocks (weighing from 2 to 5 tons) were stocked on dry land until the new site, where the work of reassembly will soon be completed, had been prepared. Specialists decided to move the temples onto the small island of Agilkia, 985 feet (300 m) from Philae, where they will be well above water level all year round. To make place for the edifices on this granite island, 900,000 tons of rock were levelled with 150 tons of dynamite. A thousand specialized workmen devoted three years to the task of disassembly. The reconstruction will take many years. The entire operation will cost no less than fifteen or twenty million dollars.

But what counts is that we can now be perfectly sure the temple of Isis, "the pearl of Egypt", will be definitively saved. It will soon rise up on its new site and be resuscitated in the light of day after a long underwater burial and a dismemberment recalling the myth of Isis and Osiris: just as Osiris's body came back to life after his limbs, mutilated by Seth and thrown into the Nile, had been brought back together one by one and reunited thanks to Isis' loving care, the temple will be reborn stone by stone in a strange modern-day Epiphany.

The temple of Kom Ombos, erected during the Ptolemaic and Roman periods, was dedicated to Horus the falcon and Sebek the crocodile. It contains quite beautiful low reliefs on which we may still see remnants of stucco and polychrome ornamentation. This profile of a goddess, caressed by the setting sun, possesses un unquestionable charm.

The Last Egyptian Cults

The last communities celebrating the Pharaonic pagan rituals found refuge on the island of Philae. These ancient rites are perpetuated in the sanctuary of Isis the Merciful until the middle of the 6th century A.D., i.e. a hundred and fifty years after Theodosius' edict had ordained the closure of all pagan temples. Three and a half thousand years had then gone by since the first dynasties established their control over the unified Nile Valley...

At Philae, thanks to the efforts of the last Egyptian priests, still capable of reading hieroglyphic, the antique ritual of the Egyptian cults holds its own against the Thebaid monks and anchorites. But the rise of Christianity is an irresistible tide, carrying all before it : and when, in 550, the temple of Isis is closed by an imperial decree issued by Justinian himself in Byzantium, we may affirm that Egyptian civilization has had its day's. The vanquishers of the Pharaonic world are neither the Assyrians, the Persians, the Greeks nor even the Roman legions, but the followers of the new religion, obeying the Gospel. With the advent of Christianity, the new symbolism of the cross replaces the keys of life on temple walls. And one of humanity's greatest civilizations falls into oblivion.

From this time forward, the sacred images and low reliefs will be vandalized. The all too sensual body of the goddess will disappear under thick coats of mortar. Her features, her tender smile full of mercy will be frenetically defaced by desert cenobites. The sanctuary's doors will be broken and opened to the mob. The holy of holies will be profaned and the statues contained in the naos thrown down and beheaded. The

King Ptolemy Neos Dionysus (about 200 B.C.), holding the whip and key of life, about to undergo ceremonial lustration. The lion-headed goddess Sekhmet offers him the key of life while falcon-headed Horus looks on. An admirable mastery of colour and shading gives life to this wall painting adorning the first hypostyle hall at Kom Ombos.

On a wall of the temple of Kom Ombos: a small falcon symbolizing the god Horus, ruler of the heavens.

The chapels occupying the furthermost part of the temple at Kom Ombos were decorated in the last days of Pharaonic Egypt. Among scenes bearing witness to a still masterly workmanship, inscriptions come to a sudden halt, as if work had been interrupted by the rise of Christianity. The last inscriptions date from the reign of Macrinus, in the 3rd century A.D.

treasury plundered, the library ransacked, the papyrus rolls burned in the hopes of abolishing the ancient wisdom of the nation of the Pharaohs. And the countless inscriptions engraved on the walls of the desecrated sanctuary will be struck dumb for centuries. These texts, in which the priests, face to face with the impending disaster, summarized Egypt's heritage, are henceforward entirely incomprehensible. And thirteen hundred years will go by from the day the last scribe, chased out of the temple, flees before the riotous mobs, until Champollion restores the faculty of speech to these documents resuming the knowledge and thought of Ancient Egypt.

Paradoxically enough, the temple of Philae converted into a church will prove to be a stronghold of Christianity where Coptic monks long hold out against Islam. As if certain sacred places were predestined, as if man's faith took up its residence at exceptional sites, Philae symbolizes more than Egypt's swan song... And it is not an insignificant fact that precisely this temple is now the object of an exemplary rescue operation.

The Legacy of Ancient Egypt

As far back as Greek times, it had become a tradition to give all branches of science Egyptian origins. The mathematicians and astronomers and even the philosophers who had not drawn their knowledge from its very sources in the temples of Memphis or Thebes, were considered unworthy of notice. The "Lives" of Pythagoras and Plato note long stays on the banks of the Nile.

Since the 5th century B.C., this tradition has been firmly maintained. The excavations of Egypt in the 18th century brought about a veritable frenzy of rediscovery and is even given a name: pyromidology. According to the enlightened theories of the pyramidologists, the great monuments (the temple of Luxor, for example, to say nothing of the three sepulchres at Giza!) contain in the form of cryptograms yet to be deciphered, all mankind's knowledge as well as the solutions to the mysteries of the universe...

A Reputation for Wisdom

To what does Pharaonic Egypt owe this reputation for wisdom and inexhaustible knowledge?

To be sure, Egyptian architecture often fills us with wonder, on account of both its aesthetic qualities and the technical feats without which it would not have been possible. While the pyramid builders managed to solve the problems of geographical location and statistical arrangement of masses, the methods employed are nonetheless wholly empirical, based on a good knowledge of building materials and simple craftiness (for example, a several hundred metre long ditch filled with water makes it possible to obtain a perfectly horizontal base!). The

The temple of Isis at Philae, submerged beneath the waters of a bay situated between the old Aswan Dam and the modern High Dam. This is all that could be seen of the monuments before the rescue operation undertaken in 1973. On the left, the first pylon. On the right, Trajan's Pavilion.

Protected from the Nile waters by a 2954 feet (900 m) long steel sheet-pile dam, the temple of Philae as it could be seen in 1974, shortly before disassembly undertaken under the auspices of UNESCO.

Trajan's Pavilion rises up among the mud banks deposited on all sides of the sanctuaries during their stay under water.

reason why the colossi could be transported to destinations hundreds of kilometres away from their places of origin was due first and foremost to the excellent organizational skills of those well versed in the tricks of the trade. It is true that the art of stonecutting is admirably mastered, but the method employed dates from prehistoric times.

How do things stand in the sphere of geometry and astronomy? To be sure, the Egyptians know how to calculate the area of a triangle and the volume of a pyramid. They subtract by complementarity and multiply by repeated duplications. But these are mere practical expedients. They even obtain a fair approximation of pi. However, they formulate no mathematical laws. They do in truth invent a more or less accurate calendar. They follow the movement of the planets and stars at the horizon. But their astronomy never goes beyond mere apparent movement: the sun and stars "rise" and "set" with respect to the fixed and motionless earth, situated at the centre of the universe.

As far as medicine goes, embalming has perhaps contributed to a better knowledge of the internal organs. Nevertheless, Egyptian physiology keeps within narrow bounds: the function of the kidneys is unknown! But fractures are well set and an efficacious pharmacopoeia is at times employed, along with a hotchpotch of magical spells.

No, however great may have been the influence of Egyptian civilization, its major contributions cannot be said to have been found in the realm of science. Egypt never surpassed Babylonia in astronomy or even in law making, having nothing to compare with Babylonia's rigorous codes.

The Pharaonic legacy is far more significant in the spheres of art, wisdom and ethics and it is not long before the extremely original language of aesthetics that the Egyptians formulated as far back as the first dynasties imposes itself on all modes of the plastic arts reaching great heights of achievement — in sculpture and official portraiture as

The second pylon of the temple of Isis at Philae: 98 feet (30 m) wide and 46 feet (14 m) high, it was decorated about 100 B.C. and bears the effigy of Neos Dionysus. The portal (centre) was raised under Euergetes II, about 135 B.C.

Detail of the goddess Hathor's portrait adorning the capitals in the mammisi at Philae. The goddess's cow-ears are clearly visible.

View of lavish Hathoric capitals. The goddess's portrait is crowned with the traditional dado. This portico surrounding the mammisi in the temple of Isis at Philae was completed under Tiberius, about A.D. 30.

well as in a sort of genre-painting portraying ordinary life, animals and the day-to-day environment.

With respect to literature, we may safely say that this civilization of scribblers and red-tape merchants, centred round the written word, was acquainted with all possible literary genres : these discoverers of writing put their invention to use in admirable religious texts, cosmogonies, hymns, prayers, invocations, oracles, but also erotic poetry, adventure stories, tales, satires, etc. But Egyptian originality most excels in the realm of esoteric wisdom. The moral code set down in writing as far back as the Old Kingdom clearly foretells biblical texts : the great hymns open the way for the Psalms.

A sense of Perfection

The music of the Nile Valley has, alas ! faded into silence. While we may admire musicians and dancers on tomb walls the absence of musical notation deprives us of all precise testimony. Nothing remains apart from the representation of all sorts of instruments, from the flute to the harp, from lutes to trumpets. Perhaps the lone vestige of this music still haunts the chants of the antique Coptic liturgy in which we may also perceive a distant echo of the language spoken by the Ancient Egyptians in days gone by...

Nonetheless, in spite of the destruction wrought by human invaders

The Pharaoh offering a sacrifice to Isis : ornamentation of a column in the courtyard of the temple of Isis at Philae.

Above :
The apse of the temple of Isis at Philae, preceding the two massive pylons. Late Egyptian architecture remains strict and rigorous even in its ultimate creations.

Trajan's Pavilion is an enormous copy of the small shrines of the sacred bark, so common during the classic era. The ornamentation is unfinished. The edifice was meant to be covered with a wooden barrel-roof or awning.

View from the second pylon at Philae: the mammisi and the west end of the first pylon.

The great temple of Isis with its many outlying shrines will be rebuilt on the small island of Agilkia, 985 feet (300 m) from Philae. An enormous mass of granite has been levelled in order to make room for the sanctuaries. Clouds of dust rise up above the work site on this tiny island where the temples will soon be reassembled out of the waters' reach.

The great colonnade of the portico erected under Augustus and Tiberius, at the dawn of the Christian era, leads to the south end of the island of Philae. In ancient times, boats moored here alongside the quays.

The cult of the priests of Philae was founded on the myth of Isis and Osiris, in high favour at the dawn of the Christian era. Ancient Egyptian rites were transformed and democratized under the influence of religions promising salvation. Osiris, king of the dead, appears here as a mummy bound in wrappings and covered with a shroud. Behind him, his wife Isis the Merciful holds the symbolic key of life.

93

and the passage of time, in spite of the mutilations suffered by so many of these works of art and the all too few in number that have survived, Egypt remains one of the most grandiose civilizations in the history of mankind.

In a sentence, the indestructable legacy of Egypt consists essentially in this sense of perfection that touches us so deeply, this love of beautiful forms, harmonious rhythms, perfect objects. Here lies the very essence of the Egyptian miracle that explains as much as anything for us the life and purpose of these men and women who lived four or five thousand years ago, their doings, anxieties and aspirations, just as if they were our own fellow men living today — as if the differences of language, religion and civilization were no more a barrier than the time gone by.

The fact that we are still thrilled at the sight of Pharaonic masterpieces is the only valid explanation for the extreme vitality of this marvellous message, the origin of which is lost in the mists of time. Egypt's main gift to mankind is nothing other than our everlasting amazement at the sight of these works of art, at the thought of their several thousand year long past.

Facing page :
On the first pylon at Philae, the sensual silhouette of the beautiful Hathor shocked Christians who converted the temple into a church in the 6th century. They covered the sculptures with coats of mortar on which they engraved Coptic religious texts. Such a protective coating preserved this admirable low relief dating from the reign of Neos Dionysus.

In the apse of the temple of Isis, the last inscriptions of Philae will soon be replaced by the cross of triumphant Christianity.

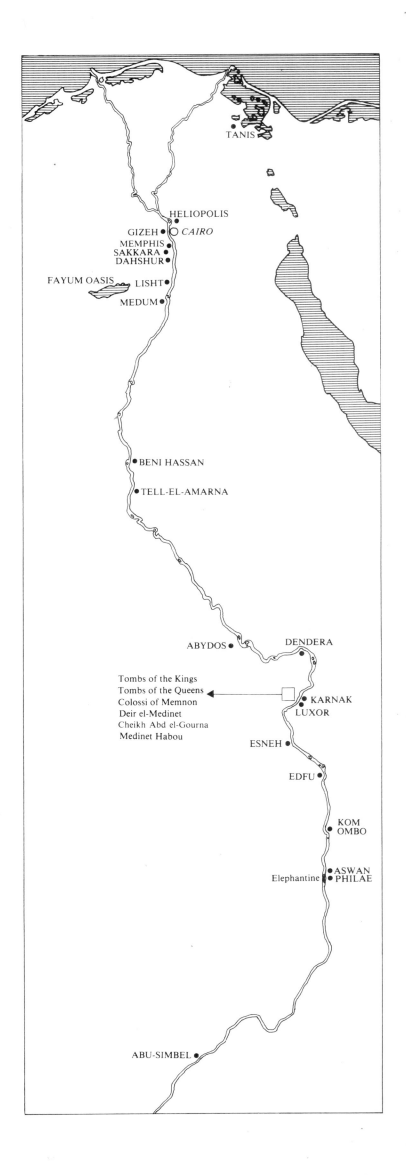

TANIS

HELIOPOLIS
GIZEH ● ○ *CAIRO*
MEMPHIS ●
SAKKARA ●
DAHSHUR ●
FAYUM OASIS   LISHT ●
MEDUM ●

● BENI HASSAN

● TELL-EL-AMARNA

ABYDOS ●   DENDERA

Tombs of the Kings
Tombs of the Queens
Colossi of Memnon
Deir el-Medinet
Cheikh Abd el-Gourna
Medinet Habou

KARNAK
LUXOR

ESNEH ●

EDFU ●

KOM
OMBO

● ASWAN
Elephantine ● ● PHILAE

ABU-SIMBEL ●